SCHOOL DINNERS

SCHOOL DINNERS

Linda Sonntag
with illustrations
in questionable taste
by **Tim Earnshaw**

SIDGWICK & JACKSON

LONDON

First published in Great Britain in 1988
by Sidgwick & Jackson Limited

Copyright © 1988 by Linda Sonntag

Designed by Tim Earnshaw

ISBN 0-283-99597-1

Photoset by Rowland Phototypesetting Limited
Bury St Edmunds, Suffolk
Printed in Great Britain by
Butler and Tanner Limited
Frome and London
for Sidgwick & Jackson Limited
1 Tavistock Chambers, Bloomsbury Way
London WC1A 2SG

CONTENTS

'That's what I call a curry . . !' rasped Nigel

INTRODUCTION

The subject of school dinners never fails to arouse strong emotions. School dinners should have been delicious (what could be more comforting to an overworked brain than a thick creamy rice pudding with a crisp brown skin on top?) but as often as not they weren't, and it is for their astonishing awfulness that they are remembered with such vivid relish. A whiff of cabbage is enough to open the floodgates of memory and reveal a vat of black leathery leaves heaving and bubbling away all morning like a vast compost heap. What could be more revolting than Flat Meat, Squashed Flies or Accident in the Alps?

This book is full of traditional recipes for the wholesome and less wholesome delights of childhood. It is hoped that it will provide people with a sane alternative to Nouvelle Cuisine.

Chapter 1

SCHOOL DINNERS

A Filling Potato Soup
Steamed Cheese Shape
Kidney Soup
Swede and Carrot Pie
Tripe and Onions
Stewed Oxtail
Stuffed Hearts
Framlingham College Faggots
Shepherd's Pie
Shrewsbury Stewed Kidneys
Marlborough Curried Mutton
Our 'Arry's Yorkshire Pudding
Eton Stew
Luscious Lissa's Liver and Bacon
Mutton Cutlets

Randal's Rumburgh Dumplings
School Dinners' Special Meat Pudding
Fairy Pudding
Radleigh Ronnie's Date Pudding
Plum Duff
Fabian's Fabulous Fig Pudding
Lemony Suet Pudding
School Dinners' Special Spotted Dick
Baked Semolina Pudding
Plain Steamed Sponge Pudding
Felsted School's Fruit Squash Jelly
Sultana Roly Poly
Jam Roly Poly
Marcia's Marmalade Pudding
Bread and Margarine Pudding

School Dinners

The school canteen was like a Roman baths. The smell of the huge grey knitted dishcloths, used to swipe the leftovers from the first sitting on to the floor, hung heavily in the air. The condensation streamed down the walls and steamed up the windows. The bad-tempered sweating dinner ladies in their rolled-up sleeves and hairnets grunted with the effort of lifting giant cauldrons with their fat red arms. The atmosphere encouraged a torrid release of the emotions that had been suppressed all morning.

School food is remembered with enthusiastic affection. Hard slabs of liver and watery wodges of mash; trays of grey roast slices laced together with shimmering gristle and wallowing in thick glutinous gravy; heaps of swede giving way as summer approached to arrangements of the outer leaves of scores of lettuces, tinged puce with the vinegar of endless beetroot.

The spectrum of textures was impressive, from the slime of tapioca through the rubbery resilience of steamed suet to the explosive brittleness of Bakewell tart. Everything culminated in the custard, solid, strong tasting and yellow. But the greatest pleasure of all was the anticipation – sitting in the classroom all morning with boiled aromas billowing in, promising fun to come.

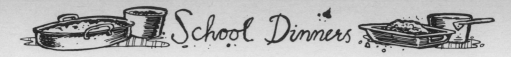

A FILLING POTATO SOUP

1½ lb potatoes

1 Spanish onion

1½ pints of white stock or water

½ teaspoon salt

Cayenne pepper

½ pint milk

1 oz cornflour

Croûtons

Wash, peel, and cut potatoes and onions into slices. Put them in a pan with the stock or water, salt and pepper. Simmer till tender. Rub through a sieve. Add the milk blended with the cornflour. Cook for 2 minutes, stirring well. Serve with croûtons of fried bread.

STEAMED CHEESE SHAPE

4 oz rice

3 gills rice or potato water

1 gill milk

1 oz cornflour

2 oz cheese, grated

Salt and pepper

Simmer the rice in the water until it is absorbed, then add half the milk. Mix the cornflour smoothly with the rest of milk, and stir into the rice. Cook gently for 2 or 3 minutes, stirring well. Mix in the cheese and plenty of seasoning, and pour into a mould. Steam for 20–30 minutes.

This can be served hot, or eaten cold with salad.

KIDNEY SOUP

1 lb ox kidney

½ lb shin of beef

Salt and pepper

1 dessertspoon flour

1 carrot

1 turnip

1 onion

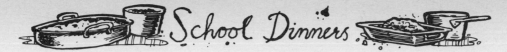

1½ oz dripping
1 quart cold water
Gravy browning
1 dessertspoon cornflour

Cut the kidney and the steak into neat pieces, and toss in seasoned flour. The vegetables should be cut up as well into thin strips. Fry all together in the hot dripping. Add the water and gravy browning, and bring to the boil. Simmer slowly for 3 hours, and then strain through a fine wire sieve.

Select the best bits of kidney, and keep them on one side. Rub the rest of the meat through the sieve, and return to the pan.

Add the cornflour, blended with a little cold water to a smooth paste. Boil for 2 minutes, stirring all the time, put in the pieces of kidney, and serve.

'Take one,' urged Humphrey insinuatingly, 'they're delicious!'

SWEDE AND CARROT PIE

½ oz butter

1 small onion, finely chopped

1 cupful mashed cooked swede

¼ cupful mashed cooked carrot

Seasoning

½ teaspoon sugar

1 egg, separated

Melt the butter in a frying-pan and add the onion. Fry for about 8 minutes, but do not let it get too brown. Beat the onion with any remaining fat into the swede and carrot. Add seasoning to taste and sugar. Beat the yolk of egg separately and mix in. Last of all, fold in the stiffly whipped white. Turn into a well greased casserole and bake in a moderate oven (Gas Mark 4, 350°F) for about 30 minutes.

TRIPE AND ONIONS

½ lb tripe

1 large Spanish onion

¾ pint milk

1 oz flour

Salt and pepper

Cut the tripe into neat pieces and blanch; cut the onion into thin slices, and put with the tripe and milk into a pan. Simmer for 2 hours. Blend the flour with a little extra milk and stir till boiling. Cook for 5 minutes longer and season.

Serve garnished with triangles of toast.

STEWED OXTAIL

1 oxtail

1 tablespoonful of dripping

½ turnip, diced

1 piece of celery, chopped

½ carrot, diced

1 onion, diced

1½ pints of stock

Bunch of sweet herbs

Blade of mace

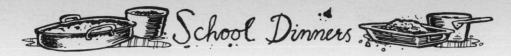

3 or 4 cloves

Peppercorns

1 dessertspoon arrowroot

Bring the tail to the boil in cold water. Drain, dry it, and cut into joints. Heat the dripping and fry the tail till well browned. Add the vegetables, then cover with stock. Add the herbs and seasoning and simmer gently for 3 hours till the meat is tender.

Lift the meat from the saucepan and strain the stock. Blend the arrowroot with a little water, add to the stock and bring to the boil, stirring; simmer gently for 5 minutes. Strain over the tail. Serve garnished with a macedoine of vegetables or green peas in small heaps.

STUFFED HEARTS

2 sheeps' or pigs' hearts

2 onions or leeks

2 small carrots

1 small turnip or swede

1½ oz cooking fat

Salt and pepper

1 heaped tablespoon flour

¾ pint vegetable stock or water

1 teaspoon mixed herbs

Stuffing

4 heaped tablespoons fresh breadcrumbs

1 tablespoon chopped parsley

1 level teaspoon mixed herbs

½ oz margarine, melted

Salt and pepper

A little milk to mix

Wash the hearts in warm water. To make the stuffing, mix all the stuffing ingredients together and add sufficient milk to bind. Season, and stuff the hearts. Slice the onions or leeks, cube the other vegetables and fry in the cooking fat. Place in a casserole and add pepper and salt. Fry the hearts until browned, lay on top of the vegetables, and season. Sprinkle the pan with flour, and stir until brown. Add the stock or water and stir until it boils. Cook for 3 minutes. Add the herbs tied up in muslin, and pour the stock round the hearts.

Cover, and cook for 1½–2 hours on the middle shelf of a very moderate oven (Gas Mark 3, 325°F). Remove the bag of herbs before serving, and cut each heart in half.

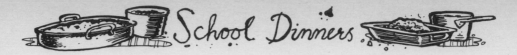

FRAMLINGHAM COLLEGE FAGGOTS

1 lb stale bread

1 lb pigs liver

¼ lb fat pork or bacon

1 lb onions, sliced

Little bunch of fresh herbs, chopped, or ¼ teaspoonful dried herbs

6 sage leaves

Salt and pepper

Pig's caul

Remove any hard crusts from the bread and cut it in small pieces. Cover it with warm water, and when quite soft drain off the water, press the bread as dry as possible and beat it smooth with a fork. Wash and dry the liver. Remove any rind from the fat pork or bacon, then cut liver and bacon into small pieces and mix with the onions. Put the mixture through a mincer.

Add the herbs to the bread and season well. Now add the minced meats, and when thoroughly mixed, form the mixture into balls.

Wash the caul and cut it in squares with scissors. Wrap each ball in a piece of caul, and pack them closely together in a baking tin. Bake in a hot oven (Gas Mark 7, 425°F) for about 45 minutes. They should be nicely browned when done. Serve hot or cold.

SHEPHERD'S PIE

1 medium-sized onion, chopped

½ oz cooking fat

1 heaped dessertspoon flour

¼ pint vegetable stock or water

1 dessertspoon Worcester sauce

Pepper and salt

½ lb cooked meat

1 lb freshly cooked potatoes

A little milk

Fry the chopped onion in the cooking fat; add the flour, cook until it browns. Add the stock or water and stir until thick. Add Worcester sauce and season well. Mince or chop the meat, mix with the gravy and half the potatoes, and place in a greased pie dish. Mash the rest of the potatoes with a little milk, spread over the meat, mark with a fork and bake for 40 minutes on the middle shelf of a moderately hot oven (Gas Mark 5, 375°F).

'So you've discovered my little secret . . .'
breathed Sir Toby menacingly

SHREWSBURY STEWED KIDNEYS

2 sheep's kidneys

¾ oz flour

Salt and pepper

1 oz butter

1 teaspoon finely chopped onion

½ pint warm water

Toast

Parsley

Skin and core the kidneys, cut into small pieces. Mix together the flour, pepper and salt, and toss the kidneys in it. Melt the butter in a stew-pan and fry the onion and kidneys till brown. Add water, stir till boiling, and simmer slowly for 30 minutes.

Serve on squares of toast. Garnish with chopped parsley.

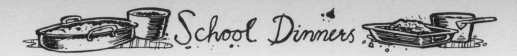

MARLBOROUGH CURRIED MUTTON

1 tablespoon desiccated coconut

2 lb neck of mutton

2 oz butter

1 onion, chopped

1 small apple, peeled, cored and chopped

1 tablespoon curry powder

2 oz flour

¾ pint stock

2 oz sultanas

1 tomato, cut in quarters

½ teaspoon sugar

½ teaspoon salt

1 tablespoon lemon juice

Boiled rice to serve

Steep the coconut in a little boiling water. Remove the bones from the meat and divide into 1″ squares. Fry the meat until brown in the butter in a pan. Remove the meat and fry the onion and apple. Sprinkle in the curry powder and flour and fry for a few minutes, then gradually add the stock, stirring to a thick smooth mixture. Turn into a casserole with the rest of the ingredients, including the water strained from the coconut. Cover with a lid and cook in the oven for 2 hours on very low (Gas Mark ¼, 250°F).

Serve in a pile with the sauce around, with a dish of boiled rice.

OUR 'ARRY'S YORKSHIRE PUDDING

¼ lb flour

Pinch of salt

1 or 2 eggs

½ pint milk

2 oz dripping

Mix the flour and salt in a bowl, add the eggs and milk gradually, and beat to a smooth batter. Allow to stand in a cool place for an hour, or as long as possible. Have the dripping very hot in a Yorkshire pudding tin, pour in the batter, and bake for 30 minutes in the middle of a moderately hot oven (Gas Mark 6, 400°F), or in a drip pan with complete meals.

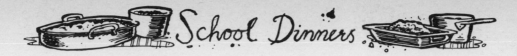

ETON STEW

8 oz stewing steak

2 oz kidney

¼ lb onions, sliced

1 heaped dessertspoon cooking fat

¾ oz flour

Water

½ lb carrots, chopped

1 heaped teaspoon mashed swede

1 heaped teaspoon mashed parsnip

1 oz chopped parsley

Salt and pepper

Cut the steak and kidney into pieces. Fry the meat and onion in the cooking fat in a saucepan, and remove. Add the flour and cook until it browns. Add water, stir until boiling and cook for 3 minutes. Lower the heat, add the meat, vegetables and parsley. Season, put on the lid and simmer for 1½ hours.

LUSCIOUS LISSA'S LIVER AND BACON

1 lb calf's liver

Flour

Salt and pepper

6 oz bacon rashers

Cut the liver into even slices ¼" thick and dip each piece into flour to which a little salt and pepper has been added. Fry the bacon, remove from the pan and fry the liver on both sides in the bacon fat. Lift out and keep hot on a dish with the bacon.

Onion rings may be fried with the liver.

To make a gravy, pour off a little of the bacon fat, add about 1 dessertspoon of flour to the remainder, stir and cook together until of a good brown colour, and then add ½ pint water and bring to boiling point while stirring. Cook for 5 minutes, adding more seasoning and gravy browning if required. Pour it round the liver and bacon.

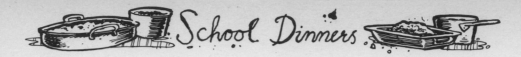

MUTTON CUTLETS

2 lb best end neck of mutton

1 egg, beaten

2 oz breadcrumbs

Pepper and salt

Frying fat

Saw off the chine bone and divide the meat into cutlets, leaving a bone to each; bare the top end of the bone about 1″. Pare off the fat and beat the cutlets, reshape, then brush over with egg and roll them in breadcrumbs seasoned with salt and pepper. Scrape all the crumbs off the bone.

Put in a basket and fry in smoking hot fat for 7 or 8 minutes. Drain on soft paper; serve in a ring, with tomato sauce poured in the centre – not over the meat; or the sauce may be served separately in a sauceboat.

RANDAL'S RUMBURGH DUMPLINGS

4 heaped tablespoons self-raising flour

1 level teaspoon baking powder

Pepper and salt

½ oz cooking fat

2 heaped tablespoons semolina

4 tablespoons water

Sieve the flour and baking powder into a basin, add pepper and salt and rub in the fat. Stir in the semolina and mix with the water to a fairly soft dough. Knead lightly on a floured board, divide and roll into dumplings and add to a boiling soup or stew. Cook for 40 minutes, or steam alone for 40 minutes and serve with brown gravy.

SCHOOL DINNERS' SPECIAL
MEAT PUDDING

6–8 oz stewing steak

1 rounded dessertspoon flour

Salt and pepper

3 carrots, chopped

3 medium-sized onions, chopped

½ pint vegetable stock or water

2 level teaspoons meat extract or 2 meat cubes dissolved in water

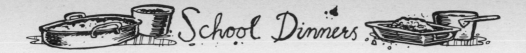

Pudding crust
4 oz self-raising flour
Pinch of salt
1 level teaspoon baking powder
½ oz cooking fat
2 heaped tablespoons semolina or suet
4 tablespoons water

To make the crust, sieve the flour, salt and baking powder into a basin, rub in the fat, and stir in the semolina or suet. Mix with the water to a fairly soft dough. Turn on to a floured board and knead lightly. Roll out two-thirds and line a greased pudding basin with it. Roll out the remainder into a circle to fit the top and put aside.

Cut up the steak and roll it in the flour, seasoning well with salt and pepper. Fill the basin with layers of meat and vegetables. Add pepper and salt and the stock or water and meat extract. Turn the pudding crust edges over the meat, and damp them. Press on the lid of crust, cover with greaseproof paper brushed with margarine and steam for 3 hours.

Gwendolyn thrust the globe artichoke into her pocket

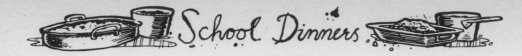

FAIRY PUDDING

1½ oz cornflour

1 pint water

2 lemons

4–6 oz sugar

Whites of 2 eggs

Yolk of 1 egg

Blend the cornflour with a little of the water to a smooth cream. Add the thinly peeled lemon rind and the lemon juice to the remainder of the water, and bring to the boil slowly. Remove the lemon rind and gradually amalgamate the cornflour and lemon juice. Add the sugar, bring to the boil and cook for 10 minutes, stirring all the time.

Put three-quarters of the mixture into a separate dish, and when slightly cool stir in the whites of the two eggs beaten to a stiff froth. Pour into a mould. To the remaining quarter of the mixture add half a gill of water and the beaten yolk of egg and bring to the boil, then allow to cool.

When both are cool, turn out the larger portion first, roughly whisk the yellow portion, and place round it.

RADLEIGH RONNIE'S DATE PUDDING

3 heaped tablespoons self-raising flour

Pinch of salt

½ level teaspoon mixed spice

½ level teaspoon baking powder

4 heaped tablespoons breadcrumbs

2 oz margarine

1 tablespoon sugar

2 oz dried dates, chopped

8 tablespoons milk

Sieve together the flour, salt, spice and baking powder, stir in the breadcrumbs, then rub in the margarine. Add the sugar and dates, and mix with the milk to a fairly soft dough. Put into a well greased basin, and steam for 1¼ hours.

Serve with custard or golden syrup.

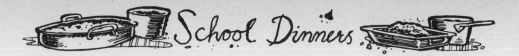

PLUM DUFF

2 oz margarine

1 tablespoon sugar

1 egg, beaten

4 oz self-raising flour

Pinch of salt

5 tablespoons milk

1 teaspoon lemon essence mixed with 2½ teaspoons water

2 lb plums bottled in syrup

2 tablespoons syrup in which plums were bottled

Cream the margarine and sugar together, and beat in the egg. Add the sifted flour and salt. Mix with the milk to a dropping consistency. Stir in the lemon and water. Put the plums in a greased pie dish with 2 tablespoons of the syrup in which they were bottled. Pour the sponge mixture on top. Bake for 40–50 minutes in a moderately hot oven (Gas Mark 5, 375°F).

FABIAN'S FABULOUS FIG PUDDING

8 oz dried figs

3 oz brown sugar

½ pint milk

1 oz flour

1 oz cornflour

½ oz baking powder

4 oz breadcrumbs

4 oz suet, chopped

Nutmeg, grated

2 eggs, beaten

Chop the figs and sugar together, and stew gently in the milk for 15 minutes. Sift the flour, cornflour and baking powder together well, put into a basin with the breadcrumbs, suet and nutmeg, and mix well together.

Stir in the stewed fig mixture, and beat in the eggs. If it is too dry add a little milk. Put into a well buttered basin. Steam or boil for 4–5 hours.

Serve with custard sauce round the pudding.

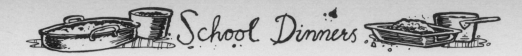

LEMONY SUET PUDDING

Suet crust

6 oz flour

2 oz suet

½ teaspoon baking powder

Salt

Water

Filling

1 or 2 eggs

4 oz sugar

Rind and juice of 1 lemon

1 oz butter, melted

Line a 1½-pint basin with the suet crust (see p. 17), reserving enough for a layer in the middle of the basin, as well as for the lid. Beat together the eggs, sugar, lemon rind and juice and the melted butter. Pour half the mixture into the basin, put in the layer of pastry, then add the remainder of the mixture. Fix on the pastry lid, cover with greased paper and steam for 2–3 hours.

SCHOOL DINNERS' SPECIAL
SPOTTED DICK

8 oz self-raising flour, or plain flour with 3 teaspoons baking powder

4 oz shredded suet

A pinch of salt

2 oz sultanas or currants

1 egg, beaten (optional)

Water, milk, or cold tea to mix

Put a large pan of water on to boil. Put an old plate at the bottom of the pan to stop the pudding catching.

Scald a pudding cloth (unbleached calico or a shirt sleeve is traditional) by dipping it in boiling water and wringing out. (Watch your hands.) Flour it well.

With a knife, mix together the flour, suet, salt, fruit and egg, if using. Add just enough liquid to make a stiff dough. Form into a rounded oblong.

Tie the pudding in the cloth, leaving a little room for it to swell. Plunge immediately in boiling water to cover. Put on the lid and boil for 2–3 hours, topping up with boiling water if necessary.

Carefully remove the cloth and serve with hot custard.

The twins always enjoyed Uncle Rupert's strange picnics

BAKED SEMOLINA PUDDING
(Quick new method)

3¾ level tablespoons semolina

2 tablespoons sugar

1 pint milk

Lemon flavouring if liked

½ oz margarine

Nutmeg

Rub a pie dish with margarine and sprinkle in the semolina and sugar. Bring the milk to the boil, pour into the pie dish and stir. Allow to stand for a minute or two, stir again, add flavouring if used, dot with the margarine, grate the nutmeg over it, and bake for 45 minutes in the lower part (second shelf from the bottom) of a moderate oven (Gas Mark 4, 350°F).

Harry told Brenda that her buns were the talk of St Percival's

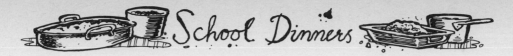

PLAIN STEAMED SPONGE PUDDING

3 oz margarine

2–3 tablespoons sugar

3 eggs, beaten

Pinch of salt

1 tablespoon milk

6 oz self-raising flour

Beat the margarine until soft, add the sugar and beat until creamy. Add the eggs, a tablespoonful at a time, and beat in each addition thoroughly before adding the next. If the mixture shows any signs of curdling beat in a little flour (sieved with the salt). When all the egg has been beaten in, add the milk and fold in the flour.

Pour into a pudding basin, rubbed with margarine, cover with grease-proof paper, and steam for 2 hours. Serve with custard.

FELSTED SCHOOL'S FRUIT SQUASH JELLY

16 tablespoons water

3 level dessertspoons powdered gelatine

2½ level tablespoons sugar

10 tablespoons fruit squash

6 oz mixed fresh fruit

Put the water, gelatine and sugar in a saucepan and stir over a low heat until the gelatine is dissolved. Do not boil. Remove from the heat, stir in the fruit squash and leave in the saucepan until beginning to set. Remove any stones, cut up the fruit and add to the jelly. Pour into a wetted mould, and leave until set.

SULTANA ROLY POLY

Suet crust (see p. 17)

2 tablespoons golden syrup

3 oz sultanas

½ teaspoon cinnamon

Make the suet crust according to the instructions on p. 17, and roll into an oblong on a lightly floured board. Heat the syrup, sultanas and cinnamon together in a saucepan, and spread the mixture evenly over the suet, leaving a margin of about ½″ all round. Damp the edges with water and roll up the

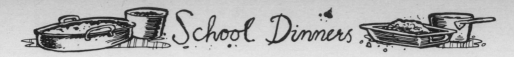

pastry, pressing the outside edges and the ends lightly down to seal. Wrap loosely in a tea towel or in greaseproof paper brushed with melted margarine; fold over the ends of the paper and steam for 1 hour.

Serve with hot syrup if liked.

JAM ROLY POLY

8 oz flour

1½ oz baking powder

4 oz suet

3 oz sugar

Milk or milk and water to mix

Jam

Sift the flour and baking powder together into a bowl. Chop the suet finely and add to the flour with the sugar. Make a well in the centre and mix to a nice dough with the milk and water. Turn on to a floured board, roll out to an oblong, spread with jam and roll up. Seal the ends firmly, place in a floured cloth, secure the ends, and plunge at once into a saucepan of boiling water. Boil for 2–2½ hours, being careful that the pudding does not go off the boil the whole time.

MARCIA'S MARMALADE PUDDING

4 oz self-raising flour

Pinch of salt

4 oz breadcrumbs

2 tablespoons marmalade

1 tablespoon sugar

1 oz margarine

2 eggs, beaten

¼ teaspoon bicarbonate of soda

1 tablespoon milk

Sieve the flour and salt, and mix with the breadcrumbs. Put the marmalade, sugar and margarine in a saucepan, and melt over heat. Allow to cool slightly, and add the eggs and the bicarbonate of soda dissolved in the milk. Stir well, and add this mixture to the flour. Mix well, put in a greased pudding basin, cover with greaseproof paper, and steam for 1 hour.

'I'll go and buy the apple sauce,' suggested Wilkes helpfully

BREAD AND MARGARINE PUDDING

4 slices stale bread

1 oz margarine

2 oz sultanas

2 tablespoons sugar

½ pint plus 6 tablespoons milk

Grease a pie dish. Spread the bread with margarine, and arrange in the pie dish, making layers of bread, fruit and sugar, ending with bread and a final sprinkle of sugar. Top with the milk and leave to soak for 30 minutes. Bake in a very moderate oven (Gas Mark 3, 325°F), on the third shelf from the top for 1½ hours.

'And if I catch you sucking Rishworth's gobstopper again I'll . . .' warned Osgood

Chapter 2
MIDNIGHT FEASTS

Coconut Whatnots
Lesbia's Hot Cheese Surprises
Carey's Caviare Sandwiches
Brains and Nuts on Toast
Cressida's Wind Balls in Syrup
Bananas in Hiding
Jolly Boys in Shirts
No-Headache Fruit Cup
Croquettes of Leftover Meat
The Ultimate Brawn
Uncle Julian's Potato Balls
Scotch Shortbread
Tacky Gingerbread
Harrow Hugo's Sausage Rolls
Scotch Breakfast Scones
Fancy Shapes in Jelly
Lionel's Queen Cakes
Winchester Willie's Chocolate Biscuits
Westminster Wilfred's Cheese Straws
The Sea Fairy's Dream
Powerful Ginger Biscuits
Golden Roe Puffs
Sandra's Stuffed Apple Fantasia

Midnight Feasts

The most delicious thing about midnight feasts is that they are forbidden. Eating in bed is a luxury permitted only to invalids under supervision and at certain times of the day. Even invalids are not allowed to eat real food in bed.

The excitement of concealing a sticky mass of chocolate wrapped up in a handkerchief under the pillow or a piece of cake in the sock drawer of the dressing table is bound to prove too much for most nocturnal revellers, and seldom does the feast take place at the allotted time – in fact it is traditional to consume everything in the first half an hour after the bedroom door has been shut or the light turned out. Use a torch to search for telltale crumbs.

Another satisfactory though more risky form of midnight feasting is preceded by a stealthy trip downstairs to raid the pantry. Avoiding detection and creaking stairs will probably be more stimulating than the food itself, which may well turn out to be just bags of flour and tins of peas.

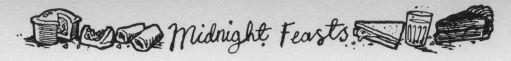

COCONUT WHATNOTS

¼ lb butter

½ lb flour

2 oz caster sugar

1 teaspoon baking powder

1 egg yolk and 1 tablespoon water beaten together

¼ teaspoonful salt

3 tablespoons desiccated coconut

Icing

5 tablespoons sifted icing sugar

1 egg white

Rub the butter into the flour; add the sugar and baking powder. Add the egg yolk and water and mix to a stiff dough with the salt. Roll out and cut into strips 3″ by 10″ long.

To make the icing, beat the egg white lightly and blend with the icing sugar. Do not over-stir or the icing will lift off the biscuits during baking. The icing should be fairly thick.

Spread the icing on the biscuits and sprinkle with coconut. Cut into strips 1″ wide. Bake for 15–20 minutes at Gas Mark 3, 325°F.

LESBIA'S HOT CHEESE SURPRISES

2 cups grated cheese

1 tablespoon butter

1 egg, beaten

Salt and pepper

Mustard

1 teaspoonful Worcester sauce

Thinly sliced bread

Bacon rashers

Mix the first 6 ingredients to a paste, then spread thickly on squares of thin bread, and top each with a thin slice of bacon. Arrange in a dish and place in the oven at Gas Mark 7, 425°F until the cheese puffs up, and the bread becomes brown.

CAREY'S CAVIARE SANDWICHES

Handle caviare with a wooden spoon only. Do not touch with metal.

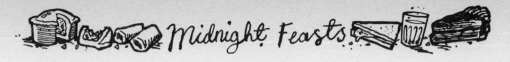

BRAINS AND NUTS ON TOAST

1 set of sheep's brains
Salt and pepper
A little milk
1 teaspoon cornflour
6 walnuts, finely chopped
4 small rounds buttered toast
1 teaspoon finely chopped parsley
A few drops lemon juice

Soak the brains in salt water for 30 minutes, skin and clean. Place in a small saucepan, cover with cold water, and bring to the boil. Boil for a few minutes and strain. Just cover with cold milk, add water, bring to the boil again, and thicken with cornflour. Add salt and pepper to taste. With a fork whip this well together. Add walnuts and beat in with the brains. Serve hot on buttered toast, garnished with finely chopped parsley and sprinkled with lemon juice.

CRESSIDA'S WIND BALLS IN SYRUP

3 heaped tablespoons flour
¼ teaspoon salt
1 dessertspoon caster sugar
1½ teacups milk
1 heaped tablespoon butter
2 eggs, beaten
Deep fat for frying
Syrup to serve

Sift the flour and salt together into a basin. Add the caster sugar. Make a well in the centre, and beat in the milk gradually. Beat well into the mixture until smooth and fairly thick (it may not be necessary to use all of the milk). Melt the butter and stir into the mixture until it thickens and is quite cold. Add the eggs and beat the mixture thoroughly. The mixture should be nearly as stiff as choux pastry mixture. Drop dessertspoonfuls into plenty of hot fat and deep fry a golden brown.

Serve with maple syrup or warmed golden syrup.

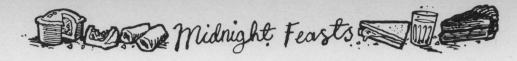

BANANAS IN HIDING

2 bananas
2 tablespoons caster sugar, plus extra for sprinkling
½ pint Yorkshire pudding batter (see p. 14)
lemon wedges

Split the bananas, halve again, roll in caster sugar and drop in Yorkshire pudding batter just before putting in the oven. See that the batter covers the bananas. Cook for 30 minutes at Gas Mark 6 or 7 (400–425°F). Serve with caster sugar and lemon quarters.

JOLLY BOYS IN SHIRTS

2½ oz butter
4 oz plus 7 oz caster sugar
4 eggs, separated
3 oz cooking chocolate, melted
4 oz ground almonds
½ oz plain biscuit, crushed
Pinch of salt
4 oz jam

Beat the butter, 4 oz sugar and 4 yolks together for 15 minutes. Add the melted chocolate and beat well. Fold in lightly the ground almonds and biscuit and pinch of salt. Pour into a square tin so that it is 1″ deep. Bake for 30 minutes in a warm oven (Gas Mark 4–5, 350–375°F).

When half-cooked, spread with jam. Have ready the stiffly beaten egg whites and lightly fold in 7 oz caster sugar. Pile on top of the cake and finish cooking very slowly – at Gas Mark 2 (300°F) for 20 minutes. The egg white must remain white and not be browned.

NO-HEADACHE FRUIT CUP

(Non-alcoholic)

1 large tin of pineapple
2 dozen oranges
1 tin passionfruit
6 pears
2 apples
1 lemon

1 large tin or 1 dozen peaches

1 dozen bottles of sparkling lemonade or pop

Peel fruits, remove pips and stones, and put all through a mincer except passionfruit. Strain through a colander; allow to stand for several hours and strain again. Add passionfruit and pour into a large punch bowl. Add lemonade just before serving.

'Go on, try just a mouthful,' pleaded Cecily

CROQUETTES OF LEFTOVER MEAT

1 oz butter or fat

1 oz flour

1 gill of water

½ lb cold minced meat

½ small onion, minced and cooked

Salt and pepper

Flour

Beaten egg

Dried breadcrumbs

Deep fat for frying

Make a very thick sauce by melting the butter and adding the 1 oz of flour. When slightly cooked add the water, stirring vigorously all the time. Add the meat and onions to the sauce. Season and spread on a plate to cool.

Make into cork-shaped pieces, then roll in flour, pepper and salt. Coat with egg and roll in the crumbs. Cook in a frying basket in very hot fat.

Serve with thick brown or tomato sauce.

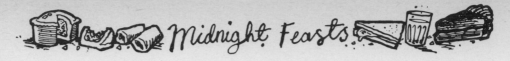

THE ULTIMATE BRAWN

4 lb shin of beef

1 sheep's head

1 cow heel, or knuckle of veal

1 pig's cheek

½ lb soup vegetables, chopped

12 allspice berries

Bunch of herbs

2 blades of mace

Peppercorns

½ nutmeg, grated

Salt and pepper

Brawn must have savoury meat such as pickled pork, and bones, such as cow heel and shin to give gelatine. Wash the meat well, removing brains from sheep's head. Chop shin and knuckle. Cover with water and bring slowly to the boil. Remove the scum. Add the vegetables, herbs and seasonings. Do not allow the vegetables to cook to a pulp and make the brawn cloudy.

Simmer till tender – about 4–5 hours with the heat very low. Lift out the meats. Strain the liquid and leave till cold. Remove the fat. Cut the meats from the bone into small pieces and place in small moulds. Reduce the stock to half by boiling rapidly. Pour it over the meat in the moulds and leave to set overnight.

The moulds may be wetted before putting the meat in, and decorated with slices of hardboiled eggs, gherkins, beetroot, etc. Turn out like jelly by dipping the mould for a second into warm water.

UNCLE JULIAN'S POTATO BALLS

1 lb cold boiled potatoes

1 tablespoon cream or milk

1 egg and 1 yolk

Salt and pepper

Flour

3 tablespoons breadcrumbs

1 oz butter

Fat for frying

Mash the potatoes, add the cream, egg yolk, pepper and salt and form into balls. Dip into flour, brush with beaten egg, toss in breadcrumbs, and fry a golden brown in hot fat.

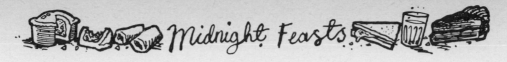

SCOTCH SHORTBREAD

8 oz butter or margarine

4 oz caster sugar

Yolk of an egg

1 lb flour

1 teaspoon baking powder

Put the butter and sugar into a basin, and beat to a cream. Make a well in the centre of the mixture and add the egg yolk. Mix the flour and baking powder together well, and add gradually to the butter and sugar, mixing thoroughly.

Turn on to a floured pastry board and work the mixture into a flat round shape. Notch the edges or place on a wooden shape or earthenware mould, and bake in a slow oven (Gas Mark 3, 325°F) for 20–30 minutes, till a nice pale brown colour. Cool on a wire tray.

TACKY GINGERBREAD

1 oz whole almonds

1 oz candied peel

1 oz treacle

3 oz brown sugar

2 oz lard or butter

8 oz flour

1 teaspoon each of ginger, cinnamon and mixed spice

A few caraway seeds, if liked

A pinch of salt

2 eggs

Scant ¼ pint milk

1 oz baking powder

Butter a 1 lb cake tin or two ½ lb cake tins. Blanch the almonds and cut the peel into small pieces. Melt the treacle, sugar and lard together.

Mix the flour and spices, almonds, peel, caraway seeds and salt together well in a bowl. Beat the eggs. Make a well in the centre of the flour mixture. Pour in the melted treacle mixture and stir well. Then add the beaten eggs, and lastly sufficient milk to make a soft batter. Beat well. Mix in the baking powder lightly, and pour at once into the cake tin or tins.

Put at once into a moderately hot oven (Gas Mark 5, 375°F). Bake for 45–60 minutes. When baked, take out of the tin and allow to cool on a wire tray.

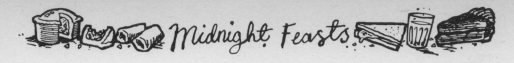

HARROW HUGO'S SAUSAGE ROLLS

8 sausages

6 oz flour

2 oz cornflour

¼ teaspoon salt

4 oz butter or margarine

Cold water

A few drops lemon juice

1 oz baking powder

Blanch the sausages, and skin them. Mix together the flour, cornflour and salt. Cut up the butter into small pieces and rub it in. Make into a very stiff paste with a little water and a few drops of lemon juice. Turn on to a floured pastry board and roll out evenly.

Fold in three and turn half way round, thus keeping the open ends towards and away from you. Roll out again. Repeat folding and rolling four times, sprinkling on half of the baking powder at the second folding, and the remainder at the fourth. After the last folding, roll it out ⅛″ thick and cut into squares.

Wet the edges of the paste all round, put a cooked sausage in the centre, and roll the paste round it, pressing it down at the ends and top with the back of a knife. Place on a greased baking sheet. Brush over with egg. Bake in a moderate oven (Gas Mark 5, 375°F) for about 20 minutes. Serve hot.

Makes 8 rolls.

SCOTCH BREAKFAST SCONES

1 lb flour

2 oz baking powder

A small teaspoon salt

About a breakfast cupful of milk (½ pint)

Mix the flour, baking powder and salt together well in a bowl. Make into a dough quickly with the milk, adding it a little at a time till you have a moderately soft dough. Do not knead more than is necessary.

Roll out flat on a floured board about ½″ thick, and cut into circles or triangles. Put at once into a hot oven or on to the griddle or hot plate sprinkled with flour. The hotter the oven the better these scones will rise. In a hot oven (Gas Mark 7 or 8, 425 or 450°F) they will be ready in 3–5 minutes. Cool on a wire tray.

Makes 12 scones.

'Cookie, Tuffy says your scones taste of sick,' mentioned Millicent

FANCY SHAPES IN JELLY

1 packet lemon jelly crystals

¾ pint boiling water

1 tablespoon vinegar

1 teaspoon onion juice

½ teaspoon salt

¼ teaspoon cayenne

Green colouring

Sprigs of cooked cauliflower

Slices of cooked potato and carrot

Slices of cucumber

Stuffed olives

Capers

½ cup grated cucumber

Crisp lettuce

Tomato slices

Make the jelly with the first 6 ingredients and colour a delicate green. Set ½″ of jelly in a wetted plain mould. Nearly fill the mould with cauliflower sprigs, fancy carrot shapes, slices of potato, cucumber, olives and capers, placing the tips of cauliflower down, arranging the vegetables artistically and adding jelly to hold in place.

Just cover with jelly and allow to set. Top up the mould with grated cucumber and the rest of the jelly. Chill and turn out on a dish garnished with plenty of crisp lettuce leaves, slices of tomato and any garnishes fancied. Serve mayonnaise separately.

It is easier when setting the jelly to stand the mould in a basin of crushed ice.

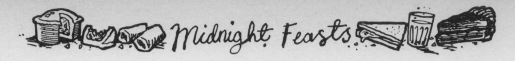

LIONEL'S QUEEN CAKES

4 oz butter or margarine

4 oz caster sugar

3 eggs

6 oz flour

½ oz baking powder

1 oz candied peel

2 oz glacé cherries

Grated rind of half a lemon

Butter 18 patty tins. Beat the butter and sugar to a cream, add the eggs one by one, beating well. Mix together the flour and baking powder, add them to the batter and mix lightly. Lastly add the candied peel, cherries and lemon rind.

Pour into the prepared tins, which should be only two-thirds filled, and bake for 20 minutes in a fairly hot oven (Gas Mark 5, 375°F). Cool on a wire tray.

Makes 12–18 cakes.

WINCHESTER WILLIE'S CHOCOLATE BISCUITS

4 oz butter or margarine

4 oz sugar

1 egg

8 oz flour

2 oz cornflour

1 oz baking powder

4 oz chocolate, grated

A little milk

1 teaspoon vanilla essence

Cream the butter and sugar together, add the egg and beat well. Sift the flour, cornflour, and baking powder together and add to mixture. Dissolve the chocolate in a little of the milk over a low heat, and add to the mixture with the vanilla essence. Use sufficient milk to make into a soft dough, and roll out to ¼″ thick. Cut out with a fancy cutter, place on a baking sheet, and bake in a moderate oven (Gas Mark 4, 350°F) for 12–15 minutes.

Makes 18 biscuits.

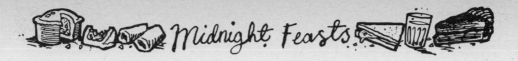

WESTMINSTER WILFRED'S
CHEESE STRAWS

2 oz flour

2 oz cornflour

2 oz butter or margarine

2 oz grated Parmesan cheese

1 oz grated Cheddar cheese

A pinch of salt, pepper, and cayenne

1 yolk of egg

Mix together the flour and the cornflour. Rub in the butter lightly. Add the grated cheeses and the seasonings. Make into a smooth paste with the egg yolk.

Roll out ¼″ thick and 6″ wide. Cut up into straws ¼″ wide. Put on a greased baking sheet and bake in a moderate oven (Gas Mark 4, 350°F) for about 20 minutes until a light yellow colour.

Serve neatly on a folded napkin.

THE SEA FAIRY'S DREAM

¼ pint milk

1 oz butter

1 oz breadcrumbs

6 oz cooked fish

1 egg

1 teaspoon HP Sauce

1 large tablespoon capers

Seasoning

Boil the milk and butter together, pour on to the breadcrumbs, and allow to soak a few minutes. Remove the bones and flake the fish finely, and mix in with the breadcrumbs and milk.

Separate the yolk and white of the egg. Beat the yolk, sauce and capers into the mixture and stir well. Season. Fold in the stiffly beaten egg white. Pour into greased moulds, cover with greased paper and steam for about 45 minutes until set.

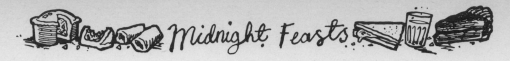

POWERFUL GINGER BISCUITS

1 tablespoon black treacle or syrup

1 tablespoon sugar

3 oz margarine

8 oz self-raising flour

1 teaspoon ground ginger

Pinch of salt

1 egg, beaten

Melt the treacle, sugar and margarine in a pan and cool slightly. Sift the flour, ground ginger and salt into a basin. Pour the melted mixture over, and mix with the egg to a stiff dough.

Roll out, cut into rounds, and bake on the second shelf of a moderately hot oven (Gas Mark 5, 375°F) for 10 minutes.

Makes 24 biscuits.

GOLDEN ROE PUFFS

4 soft herring roes

Milk

Salt and pepper

½ oz butter or margarine

½ oz flour

Cayenne pepper

Lemon juice

1 tablespoon breadcrumbs

½ lb rough puff pastry

Wash the roes. Place them in a small casserole and just cover with milk. Add salt and pepper. Place the lid on the casserole and cook in the oven for 30 minutes at Gas Mark ½ (250°F).

Melt the butter in a small saucepan. Add the flour and cook together for a minute. Add the milk from the roes. Stir and boil to make a thick sauce. Beat up the roes and add to the cooled sauce. Mix well, adding more salt and pepper, cayenne pepper and lemon juice to taste, and the breadcrumbs if the mixture is not sufficiently thick.

Roll out the pastry to an oblong strip about ⅛″ thick. Cut the strip in half. Spread the roe paste on one half and without stretching, place the other strip of pastry over the paste. Cut across into strips or triangles. Place on a baking sheet, brush with egg and bake for 15 minutes at Gas Mark 8 (450°F).

'It really is the last, sod it!' slurred Beatrice

SANDRA'S STUFFED APPLE FANTASIA

2 pork sausages
4 large cooking apples
2 tablespoons water
1 dessertspoon tomato ketchup
1 teaspoon sugar (optional)
2 rashers bacon

Boil the sausages for 10 minutes, cool and then remove the skins. Wash the apples and remove the cores and fill the centres with sausagemeat. Put them on a baking sheet and add 2 tablespoons water mixed with the tomato ketchup. Sprinkle the apples with the sugar if they are very sour.

Bake in a moderate oven (Gas Mark 4, 350°F) and when almost tender place a piece of bacon on the top of each and continue baking until it is just crisp.

Nigel had the horrible feeling that a prank was being played on him

Chapter 3

THE PICNIC HAMPER

Grantham Gingerbreads
Cookie's Sunshine Cracks
Asparagus Logs
Fairy Toadstools
Prefect's Perfect Pickled Onions
The Chums' Cold Water Ginger Beer
Benenden Boiled Ham
Remove's Raised Pork Pie
Rugby Rabbit Pie
The Caretaker's Wife's Cornish Pasties
School Dinners' Special Apple Pie
Heidi's Swiss Roll
A Good Salad
Millfield's Macaroons
Matron's Meat Mould
Miss's Melting Moments

The Picnic Hamper

A picnic hamper should be large, with a handle each side – it will need two strong people to carry it because it will be weighed down with good things. A cardboard box with a precarious bottom and a bread knife sticking out at a rakish angle will do as an alternative. You will get most pleasure from taking as little aluminium furniture with you as possible. A cloth should be spread in a shady spot free of thistles, stubble and sharp stones. There will be a babbling brook for the washing of plates, for paddling and fishing.

Cooking on a primus stove is far less fun than frying an egg and a couple of rashers on a hot stone. First build a fire (well away from bracken and other combustibles), then select a large flat stone and bury it in the embers for a few minutes. When it is good and hot, dust off the ashes and lay on a couple of rashers. Let them sizzle merrily on one side, turn them over and break the eggs on top. Result: a perfectly cooked 'B&E'.

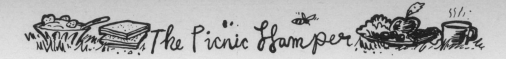

GRANTHAM GINGERBREADS

½ lb butter

1½ lb sugar

A little lemon essence

1 oz ground ginger

3 eggs

1½ lb flour

1 teaspoon baking powder

Cream the butter and sugar, add the lemon essence, ginger and eggs and beat well. Add the flour mixed with the baking powder, and work into a stiff mixture. Form into very small round balls, flatten a little, and bake on a greased baking sheet for 20 minutes at Gas Mark 4 (350°F). Makes masses!

COOKIE'S SUNSHINE CRACKS

1 tablespoon butter

1 cup sugar

2 eggs

2 cups rolled oats

1 teaspoon baking powder

Pinch of salt

Vanilla essence

Cream the butter and sugar, add the beaten eggs, oats, baking powder and salt, with a few drops of vanilla. Drop in teaspoonfuls on a greased baking tray, leaving space for spreading. Bake at Gas Mark 4 (350°F) for 10–12 minutes.

ASPARAGUS LOGS

2 oz flour plus a little extra

Salt and cayenne pepper

1 teaspoon butter

1 teaspoon grated cheese

1 dessertspoon Parmesan cheese

Beaten egg

One bunch or tin of cooked asparagus tips

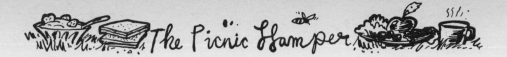

Breadcrumbs

Fat for deep frying

Sift the flour, salt and cayenne. Rub in the butter and half the cheese. Mix with a very little water to a stiff dough and roll out very thinly. Cut into pieces 1″ × 3″. Brush with egg, and put a short piece of asparagus on each. Sprinkle with salt, cayenne and the remaining cheese, and roll the pastry neatly around the asparagus. Dip in flour, egg and breadcrumbs and deep-fry until golden brown. Serve hot.

FAIRY TOADSTOOLS

Hardboiled eggs, shelled

Anchovies or gherkins

Tomatoes

Cream, stiffly beaten

Lettuce leaves

Cut the tops from the eggs and carefully remove the yolks. Cut a small piece from the bottom of each egg, just enough to make it stand firmly. Pound the yolks with the anchovies or minced gherkins, to which you can add salt and pepper, and fill the eggs.

Cut a rounded end from each of a corresponding number of tomatoes, drain, and place one slice on each egg. Pipe small spots or dots of cream over the tomato tops and serve standing on a bed of finely shredded lettuce.

Note: only suitable for picnics in the back garden. Would squash if transported in a hamper. Adds a touch of rustic sophistication to a patio brunch.

PREFECT'S PERFECT PICKLED ONIONS

2 pints of shallots, or very small onions

Salt

Enough vinegar to cover

¼ lb whole mixed pickling spice

Peel the shallots or onions and place them on a large china dish, sprinkle with salt and leave for 12 hours. Pack into jars and add the vinegar, which has been boiled and allowed to cool, together with the spices. Seal well and store in a dry place.

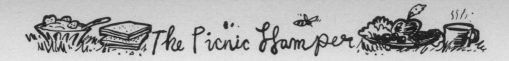

— THE CHUMS' COLD WATER GINGER BEER —

2 lb sugar

2 tablespoons each cream of tartar and ground ginger

1 teaspoon essence of lemon

2 gallons cold water

1 small cup of yeast

Stir all together well, and stand overnight. Strain and bottle. The ginger beer will be ready for drinking in 2 or 3 days.

———— BENENDEN BOILED HAM ————

1 ham

1 teaspoon pickling spice

4 oz brown sugar

Brown breadcrumbs

Cloves

Soak the ham for 12 hours. Boil very gently in fresh water to cover, allowing 25 minutes to 1 lb, and adding pickling spice and sugar to the water. When cooked peel off the skin, roll the ham in brown breadcrumbs to cover, and stud with cloves.

Leave the ham soaking in the cooking water till cold.

———— REMOVE'S RAISED PORK PIE ————

Pastry

¼ pint (1 gill) hot water

5 oz lard or suet

Salt

12 oz flour

Filling

½ lb pork, leg for preference

½ lb sausage meat

¼ teaspoon pepper

½ teaspoon salt

A pinch of mixed herbs if liked

Beaten egg

Boil the water and lard together with a teaspoonful of salt. Make a well in the centre of the flour and add the liquid. Knead well until the dough is soft. Roll out the pastry and line a greased pie mould or cake tin with about ⅔ of it.

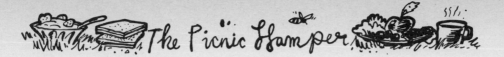

Cut the meat into cubes and add sausage meat, seasoning, and 1 table-spoon water. Put the filling into the pastry case. Brush the edges of the pastry with beaten egg. Roll out the remaining pastry to fit the top and put it on. Make a vent in the centre of the pie. Decorate with pastry leaves made from any leftovers. Brush the whole with beaten egg and bake at once at Gas Mark 8 (450°F) for 30 minutes, then lower the heat to Gas Mark 5 (375°F) and cook for a further hour.

'Who ordered the Baked Alaska?' snarled the stranger

RUGBY RABBIT PIE

1 rabbit

1–2 bacon rashers

2 onions

½ oz cooking fat

Salt and pepper

1 level dessertspoon flour

½ pint water

1 heaped teaspoon chopped parsley

Pastry made with ½ lb self-raising flour, see p. 46

Wash and joint the rabbit, cut the bacon into pieces, slice the onions, and fry all lightly in the fat. Transfer to a casserole and season. Cook the flour in the fat remaining in the pan until it bubbles, add the water and parsley and stir till boiling. Pour this over the rabbit, put on the lid and cook for 1¼ hours in the middle of a moderate oven (Gas Mark 4, 350°F) or until the rabbit is tender.

Remove the lid and allow to cool. Make the pastry according to the instructions on p. 46, cover the pie and bake for a further 30–35 minutes on the third shelf of a fairly hot oven (Gas Mark 6, 400°F).

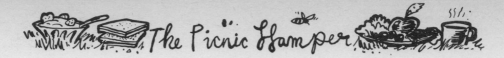

THE CARETAKER'S WIFE'S
CORNISH PASTIES

½ lb steak

1 potato

1 onion

Pepper and salt

¾ lb shortcrust pastry (see below)

Cut the meat and vegetables into small cubes; season with pepper and salt. Make the pastry according to the instructions below and divide into 4 or 5 pieces. Roll each to a circle about ⅙″ thick. Divide the filling between the circles of pastry, dampen the edges, and gather them together to make a join down the middle of each pasty. Pinch well together and curl over the joined edges. Bake on a greased baking sheet for 50 minutes at Gas Mark 5 (375°F).

SCHOOL DINNERS' SPECIAL APPLE PIE

1½ lb apples

¼ pint water

1 tablespoon lemon squash (optional)

Cloves

2 rounded tablespoons sugar

Shortcrust pastry

6 heaped tablespoons self-raising flour

Pinch of salt

2–2½ oz margarine

2 tablespoons water

Peel, core and slice the apples and cook with the water, lemon squash, cloves and sugar for 3 minutes. Turn into a pie dish and cool.

To make the pastry, sieve the flour and salt together, rub in the margarine, and mix to a stiff paste with the water. Roll out thinly on a floured board. Dampen the rim of the dish, cover with a strip of pastry, and dampen the pastry. Cover the pie with the pastry, press down, trim and flute the edges. Make a hole in the centre, and bake for 30–35 minutes on the second shelf of a fairly hot oven (Gas Mark 6, 400°F).

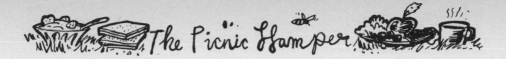

HEIDI'S SWISS ROLL

3 eggs

3 oz caster sugar

2 oz flour

½ oz baking powder

1 tablespoon hot water

¼ teaspoon vanilla essence

2 tablespoons jam, warmed

Butter and paper an oblong, flat baking tin. Whisk the whites of the eggs to a stiff froth, then add the yolks one at a time, beating well. Beat in the sugar till dissolved. Mix together the flour and baking powder, and add them with the hot water and vanilla. Mix all lightly.

Pour into the prepared tin and bake in a hot oven (Gas Mark 6, 400°F) for about 10 minutes. Turn out on to a sugared paper. Spread with jam and roll up.

A GOOD SALAD

1 lettuce

Mustard-and-cress or watercress

A slice of onion

2 or 3 tomatoes

A small beetroot

1 hardboiled egg

Cold potatoes

Any cold cooked vegetables

2 slices pineapple

Salt and pepper

Salad oil

Vinegar

Wash the lettuce and cress and shake in a salad basket or a cloth to dry. Rub the salad bowl with the onion. Tear up the lettuce and make a bed of it in the bowl. Skin and slice the tomatoes and beetroot. Slice or chop the egg, cold potatoes, cooked vegetables and pineapple and arrange loosely in the bowl. Sprinkle well with salt and pepper. Pour over the whole, 3 tablespoonfuls of oil to every 1 of vinegar.

With salad spoons carefully mix up the contents of the bowl without bruising the lettuce. A few small lettuce leaves may be arranged daintily on the top.

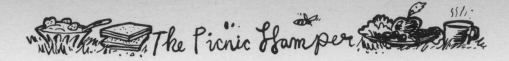
MILLFIELD'S MACAROONS

Shortcrust pastry (see p. 46)

1 egg

¾ oz cornflour

4 oz caster sugar

4 oz ground almonds

½ oz butter or margarine, melted

3 tablespoons jam

Prepare the shortcrust pastry according to the instructions on p. 46 and line one dozen greased patty tins with it. Beat up the egg and mix in the cornflour. Add the sugar, work in the ground almonds and the butter. Mix all together. Put a teaspoonful of jam into each patty tin, cover with the almond mixture and bake in a hot oven (Gas Mark 6 or 7, 400–425°F), for 15 minutes. When ready, remove from tin and lay on a wire tray to cool.

Makes 12 tartlets.

MATRON'S MEAT MOULD

1 or 2 hardboiled eggs, sliced

2 oz cooked ham, sliced

1 lb cooked chicken, rabbit or veal

1 teaspoon chopped parsley

The rind of about ½ lemon, grated

A little grated nutmeg

½ oz gelatine*

1 pint of stock

Seasoning

Dampen a mould or cake tin and line as far as possible with the egg and ham cut in slices ¼" thick. Fill the mould with the meat cut into small pieces and mixed with the parsley, lemon rind and nutmeg. Dissolve the gelatine in the stock and season well. Pour into the mould, cover with greased paper and bake for 1 hour at Gas Mark 3 (325°F). Allow to cool.

When cold, dip into water just hot enough to bear the hand in, turn out and serve with salad.

*If the stock is liquid and not jellied, allow ¾ oz gelatine in place of ½ oz.

'Which of you minxes put this Stilton in Miss Manly's underwear drawer?' quizzed Imelda briskly

MISS'S MELTING MOMENTS

6 oz butter or margarine

3 oz caster sugar

2 eggs

8 oz cornflour

1 oz baking powder

Flavouring of lemon or vanilla

Butter 18 small patty tins. Cream the butter and sugar together. Beat up the eggs, and add them alternately with the cornflour until both are used up. Last of all, add the baking powder and flavouring. Put a teaspoonful of the mixture into each of the patty tins. Bake for 10 minutes in a hot oven (Gas Mark 6, 400°F).

Makes 16–18 cakes.

'Shrove Tuesdays are a pain in the backside!' vouchsafed Gaylord

Chapter 4

CUSTARD PIES
(AND OTHER MISSILES)

Snowballs
Lemon Sago 'New Forest'
Roedean Rock Buns
Ice Cream School Treat
Sadista's Chocolate Ice
Cranleigh Custard Pies
Lemon Snow
Sharon's Lovely Waffles
Oriel's Orange Jelly
Trifle 'Doreen'
Gordonstoun Gooseberry Fool
Stoneyhurst Scones
Stowe Spiced Tea Buns
Grand Slam Granite Cakes
Remedial Rhubarb Meringues
Summer Pudding
Castle Puddings
Lamingtons
Cornflour Blancmange 'Claustrophobia'
St Bunfleet's Baked Custard

Custard Pies (and Other Missiles)

Where food, glorious food and mud, glorious mud combine is in the un-alloyed pleasure of getting hold of a custard pie and flinging it with all your might to land splat in the middle of a friend's face. Custard pies are almost as good to receive as they are to send winging on their way through a party atmosphere. Shaking dollops of custard on to the floor, licking it up, spitting it out, smearing it into your hair and hurling it back at your attacker are an essential part of the fun. The idea is to make as much mess as you can, which should be quite a considerable amount more than you achieved when you were in your high chair enjoying the same thing.

This chapter features two types of edible missile: sloppy ones and hard ones. Be warned that Granite Cakes, Rock Buns etc. can cause considerable damage, especially if you have a good aim.

51

SNOWBALLS

10 oz loaf sugar (or granulated)

1 gill water (or orange water)

1 dessertspoon glucose (weight about 1 oz)

¾ oz gelatine

1 gill water to dissolve gelatine

A few drops vanilla essence

Whites of 3 eggs

2 oz icing sugar

Boil the loaf sugar, water and glucose to 260°F in a saucepan. Meanwhile melt the gelatine in one gill of water in another saucepan. Add the vanilla essence to the gelatine. Beat the egg whites stiffly. When ready, pour the contents of both saucepans into one large saucepan. Add the stiffly beaten egg white and beat with a whisk until the mixture is stiff. Then beat with a wooden spoon until it will stand up in the mixture unsupported. Leave the mixture in the basin for 30 minutes. Turn on to a marble slab or meat dish. Sprinkle with icing sugar. Leave about 1 hour exposed to air. Press in the icing sugar. Cut into shapes.

LEMON SAGO 'NEW FOREST'

3 tablespoons sago

1 pint water

1–2 lemons (rind of 1, juice of 2)

1 tablespoon honey or golden syrup

3 tablespoons sugar

Wash the sago then soak in the water for an hour. Add the lemon rind and juice and heat, stirring, until boiling and clear. Add the honey and sugar, mix well, pour into a wetted pie dish. Cook for 1½ hours at Gas Mark 1 (275°F). Serve hot or cold.

ROEDEAN ROCK BUNS

½ lb flour

1 teaspoon baking powder

A pinch of salt

3 oz sugar

3 oz butter

3 oz currants

1 oz candied peel, chopped

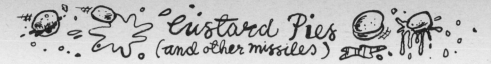

Custard Pies
(and other missiles)

1 egg, beaten
2 tablespoons milk

Sift the flour, baking powder, salt and sugar into a bowl, rub in the butter, and add the currants and candied peel. Mix stiffly with the egg and milk, place in rough heaps on a greased baking sheet, and bake for 20 minutes at Gas Mark 5 or 6 (375–400°F).

The chums packed everything they'd need for the picnic

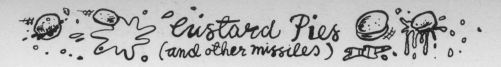

ICE CREAM SCHOOL TREAT

1 oz cornflour

1 pint milk

4 oz caster sugar

2 eggs, separated

½ pint whipped cream

Vanilla, coffee or lemon flavouring

Blend the cornflour with a small quantity of the milk till smooth, then add the rest and put it into a saucepan with the sugar. Boil for 3 minutes, stirring all the time, then add the yolks of eggs, off the heat, and cook gently for a moment. Let this cool. Stir in the whipped cream and the whites of eggs stiffly beaten. Flavour to taste with vanilla, coffee essence, or lemon juice. A teaspoonful of maraschino can be used if a wine flavouring is desired. Freeze and serve.

SADISTA'S CHOCOLATE ICE

1 oz cornflour

1 pint milk

2 oz caster sugar

4 oz chocolate, grated

½ teaspoon vanilla essence

Blend the cornflour with a small quantity of the milk till smooth, then add the rest of the milk and put it into a saucepan with the sugar. Cook for 3 minutes, stirring all the time. Add the grated chocolate, dissolved in a little hot milk. Allow the mixture to cool, add the vanilla essence, and freeze.

CRANLEIGH CUSTARD PIES

Shortcrust pastry (see p. 46)

½ pint milk

2 teaspoons sugar

2 eggs, beaten

¼ teaspoon vanilla essence

Nutmeg

Make the pastry, following the recipe on p. 46, cut into rounds, and line small greased patty tins. Place screwed-up greaseproof paper in each to prevent the pastry rising and bake on the second shelf of a moderately hot

oven (Gas Mark 6, 400°F) for 10 minutes.

Meantime, make the filling. Bring the milk and sugar to the boil, and pour it over the eggs, stirring all the time. Add the vanilla. Remove the pastry cases from the oven, three-quarters fill each tart, grate nutmeg on top of each, and bake for a further 15 minutes at the same heat.

Makes 24 pies.

LEMON SNOW

1 pint milk

1½ tablespoons cornflour

½ cup sugar

2 large lemons

2 egg whites

Heat the milk; stir in the cornflour. Add the sugar and stir until boiling. Cook for 2 minutes and stir until cool. Add the juice of 1½ lemons, stir well. Add the stiffly beaten egg whites and stir in lightly until no streaks remain. Cut the half lemon into thin slices and line a wetted mould. Pour in the mixture. Put in a cool place to set.

SHARON'S LOVELY WAFFLES

2 eggs

½ pint milk

8 oz flour

½ teaspoon salt

2 tablespoons baking powder

6 oz butter, melted

Separate the yolks from the whites of the eggs. Beat the yolks with the milk. Sieve the flour, salt and baking powder into a basin, make a well in the centre, and stir in the beaten egg yolks and milk, and the melted butter. Beat well, and just before the batter is ready to be cooked fold in the stiffly beaten whites of eggs.

Heat a waffle iron thoroughly, brush with a little oil. Pour on just enough batter to cover. Hold the handles ½″ apart at the base for a few seconds, to allow the batter to rise slightly, then close the iron down tightly. After 2 minutes turn the iron, and cook for a further 2 minutes.

Serve with warmed maple syrup.

ORIEL'S ORANGE JELLY

2 oranges
2 oz lump sugar
5 oz caster sugar
2½ oz cornflour
1½ pints water
1 lemon

Rub down the rinds of the oranges with the lump sugar, and scrape off the bits of sugar that stick to the rind. Put these into a saucepan with the caster sugar. Mix the cornflour to a smooth cream with a little of the water from the 1½ pints. Pour the rest of the water into the saucepan and bring to the boil. Remove the saucepan from the heat. Pour the mixed cornflour slowly into it, stirring vigorously. Add the juice of the two oranges and the lemon. Bring to the boil again and boil well for 3 minutes. Pour into a mould and cool. When cold, turn out and serve with whipped cream.

TRIFLE 'DOREEN'

4 sponge cakes
2 tablespoons jam
4 tablespoons fruit
Golden syrup
1¼ oz cornflour
1 pint milk
1 egg, separated
1 oz caster sugar
6 sweet almonds, shredded

Cut the sponge cakes across, and put a good layer of jam and fruit between them. Then pile them together in a glass dish, and pour the syrup over them. Blend the cornflour with the milk, and boil for 10 minutes, stirring all the time. Take off the heat and stir in the egg yolk and sugar. Cook for a moment, then pour it over the sponge cakes. Stud the almonds over the dish. Beat the egg white to a stiff froth. Put a little milk to boil in a small saucepan, and when boiling drop in spoonfuls of the egg white. Let them poach for half a minute, and put this white rock of egg daintily here and there on the trifle. Serve cold.

'Powdered rhino horn!' ejaculated Uncle Ernest, 'That's the secret ingredient!'

GORDONSTOUN GOOSEBERRY FOOL

1–1½ pints gooseberries
4 oz sugar
½ teacup water
2 oz cornflour
1 pint milk
2 eggs
1 oz caster sugar

Prepare the gooseberries and stew them with the sugar and the water till tender, then rub through a fine sieve. Blend the cornflour with a little of the milk; bring the rest of the milk to the boil. When almost boiling, stir in the blended cornflour and the gooseberry pulp and stir till it boils. Beat up the eggs with the caster sugar, add to the pudding and boil for 3 minutes. Pour into a glass dish and serve cold.

Custard Pies (and other missiles)

STONEYHURST SCONES

8 oz self-raising flour

¼ teaspoon salt

1 oz margarine

About ¼ pint water

Sieve the flour and salt together, rub in the margarine and mix to a fairly soft dough with water. Turn on to a floured board, knead and roll to a thickness of ½″. Cut into shapes, place on a greased baking sheet, and bake for 20 minutes on the second shelf of a hot oven (Gas Mark 7, 425°F). Cut open while hot and spread with margarine.

Makes 8 scones.

STOWE SPICED TEA BUNS

8 oz self-raising flour

A pinch of salt

½ teaspoon ground ginger

½ teaspoon mixed spice

1 tablespoon sugar

3 oz margarine

1 tablespoon syrup

6 tablespoons milk

1 egg, beaten

Sieve the flour, salt, ginger and spice into a basin, and add the sugar. Melt the margarine and syrup, cool and mix with the milk and egg. Stir into the flour and beat for 2 minutes. Three-quarters fill greased bun tins with the dough, and bake on the second shelf of a moderately hot oven (Gas Mark 5, 375°F) for 20 minutes. Makes 14 buns.

GRAND SLAM GRANITE CAKES

8 oz self-raising flour

A pinch of salt

3 oz margarine

3 tablespoons sugar

2 oz sultanas, currants etc.

A few drops lemon essence

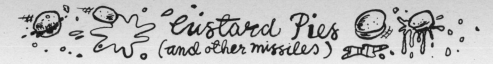

2 eggs, beaten

1 tablespoon milk

Sieve the flour and salt together and rub in the margarine. Add the sugar, fruit and lemon essence and mix to a stiff dough with the eggs and milk. Place in tablespoonfuls well apart on a greased baking sheet and bake for 20–25 minutes on the second shelf of a fairly hot oven (Gas Mark 6, 400°F).

Makes 9 cakes.

——— REMEDIAL RHUBARB MERINGUES ———

1½ lb rhubarb

6 oz plus ½ oz sugar

A strip lemon rind

3 cloves

2 egg whites

Red colouring

Stew the rhubarb with the 6 oz sugar, lemon rind and cloves until tender. Remove the lemon and cloves and beat the rhubarb with a fork till smooth. Stiffly beat the egg whites and divide in half. Add a few drops of red colouring to half the egg white, fold this into the rhubarb and pile it into a deep dish. Fold the ½ oz of sugar into the rest of the white, put it into a forcing bag and decorate the top. Set the meringues in a low oven (Gas Mark ½, 250°F) for a few minutes.

——— SUMMER PUDDING ———

1 lb soft fruit (raspberries etc.)

½ pint water

2–3 tablespoons sugar

5 slices stale bread spread with margarine

Wash the fruit and cook with the water and sugar until soft. Line a greased pudding basin with thin slices of bread, margarined side inwards. Cut a fairly thick round to fit the bottom, and place with margarined side upwards. Pour in half the fruit and juice, arrange a fairly thick layer of bread and margarine in the centre, pour in the remainder of the fruit and juice, and cover with another thick layer of bread and margarine, with the spread side downwards. Place a saucer on top, and on this place a heavy weight. Leave overnight, and turn out very carefully. Serve cold, with cold custard sauce, if liked.

CASTLE PUDDINGS

2 oz margarine

2 heaped tablespoons sugar

2 eggs, beaten

5 heaped tablespoons self-raising flour

A pinch of salt

2 tablespoons milk

Beat margarine and sugar until soft. Beat in the eggs a little at a time with some sieved flour and salt, until all the egg is added. Stir in the milk, fold in the rest of the flour. Three-quarters fill greased dariole or small moulds, and bake for 20 minutes on the third shelf of a moderately hot oven (Gas Mark 5, 375°F). Serve with hot jam.

Makes 8 puddings.

LAMINGTONS

3 eggs

3 oz butter

1 cup sugar

½ cup milk

Vanilla essence

2 cups self-raising flour

Icing

½ lb icing sugar

1 tablespoon cocoa plus 2 tablespoons hot water, or 2 tablespoons coffee essence

1 teaspoon lemon juice

1 teaspoon melted butter

½ cup jam

Desiccated coconut

Beat the eggs, butter and sugar to a cream. Add half the milk gradually with the vanilla essence, then the well-sifted flour and the rest of the milk. Mix well. Turn into a square cake tin lined with greased paper. Bake in a moderate oven (Gas Mark 4–5, 350–375°F) for 30–40 minutes.

The cake must be one day old before icing. To make the icing, mix together the sifted icing sugar, cocoa, lemon juice, butter and water till smooth (extra water may be necessary). Warm slightly over the heat but do not boil.

Cut the cake into small squares, split and put jam between. Pour the icing over the cake quickly and roll the cake in the coconut. An easy way of doing this is to hold the pieces of cake on a fork and pour the icing over with a spoon. Toss the iced cakes in the coconut until coated.

'Damn your naturist weeny roasts!' gritted Trubshaw

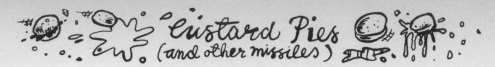

Cornflour Blancmange 'Claustrophobia'

2½ oz cornflour
2 pints best milk
1 teaspoon butter or margarine
A pinch of salt

Mix the cornflour to a smooth cream with a little of the milk. Heat the rest of the milk to boiling point in a large enamelled saucepan. Remove from heat. Pour the mixed cornflour slowly into the heated milk, stirring vigorously. Add the butter and salt. Then boil well for 10 minutes (by the clock) stirring all the time. Pour into a quart mould. When cold, turn out and serve.

If desired to eat with the chill off, re-heat gently in the mould before the fire or in a very gentle oven. Then turn out and serve.

How to serve a blancmange
A blancmange made according to this recipe should be turned out on to a glass dish, and may be served plain with milk or cream and sugar; or with any sweet sauce round the dish; or with stewed fruit placed round the dish, or served separately; or, again, with jelly or jam, or any sort of preserved fruit.

Caramel sauce for blancmange

4 oz loaf sugar
½ pint water

Put the sugar and one gill of the water into an old black saucepan, and boil till it becomes a golden brown colour. Then add the other gill of water, and boil for 2 minutes more. When cold, pour round the blancmange.

St Bunfleet's Baked Custard

1 pint milk
2 eggs
A pinch of salt
1 oz sugar
Flavouring

Heat the milk. Beat up the eggs with a pinch of salt. Pour the milk hot, not quite boiling, on to the eggs while beating. Strain into a greased pie dish. Add sugar and flavouring, if liked. Bake in the middle of the oven at Gas Mark 1 (275°F) for 50 minutes.

Chapter 5

EATING BETWEEN MEALS

A-Level Brandy Snaps
Pilthrochy Shortbread
Darren's Pickled Damsons
Auntie's Neenish Cakes
Dago Cakes
Rose Fairy Cakes
Bloater Biscuits
Stewed Eels
O-Level Jam Tart
Hortensia's Special Bannocks
Mabel's Eggless Nutties
Banana Fritters
Chocolate Pudding
Examination Potato Cakes
Chelsea Buns
Doughnuts 'Millicent'
Rhoda's Raspberry Buns
CSE Sardine Balls

Eating Between Meals

Eating between meals means stuffing yourself with things you like so that you don't have to – indeed can't – eat the things you don't like which are served up at meal times. It means a diet of gobstoppers, toffee and chocolate, cakes, fudge, lollies, pop and ice cream. It is not good for you, it gives you spots and black teeth and it damages your relationship with your parents and others in authority, but it does mean that you can cut out boring things like meat and vegetables and that you don't have room to eat your crusts up. If you have a very big appetite, of course, you can eat between meals without anyone ever finding out – in this case you will simply get fatter and fatter.

A-LEVEL BRANDY SNAPS

3 oz golden syrup

3 oz butter

3½ oz flour

3½ oz caster sugar

1 teaspoon ground ginger

Juice of ½ lemon

1 teaspoon brandy or vanilla essence

1 teaspoon grated lemon rind

Melt the syrup and butter together. Add the sifted flour, sugar, ginger and flavourings, and stir till free of lumps and like unbeaten cream. Drop in teaspoonfuls on greased baking trays, leaving a good space between and bake at Gas Mark 4–5 (350–375°F) until the surface is lacy and dry (about 6–8 minutes).

Roll quickly while hot (otherwise they will harden and become too brittle to handle), and fill with unsweetened stiffly beaten cream when cold.

PILTHROCHY SHORTBREAD

7 oz butter

8 oz plain flour

1 oz ground rice

3 oz caster sugar

½ oz coarsely chopped almonds

1 oz mixed peel

Rub the butter into the dry ingredients, and work into a smooth consistency. Work into a ½″ thick circle with the hands. Pinch the edges to decorate and put on a greased baking sheet. Bake for 50 minutes at Gas Mark 3–4 (325–350°F).

DARREN'S PICKLED DAMSONS

Select 6 lb firm sound damsons and allow:

3 lb sugar

1 pint vinegar

1 teaspoon cloves

1 or 2 oz root ginger

2 or 3 blades mace

1 teaspoon allspice

1 teaspoon peppercorns

Sprinkle half the sugar over the well washed, drained fruit, and allow to stand for 2–3 hours. Boil the vinegar with the rest of the sugar and the other ingredients for a few minutes. Cool. Add the damsons and juice, and heat very gently without boiling for 8 minutes. Lift the fruit out of the syrup and pack in hot jars. Boil the syrup and pour it over the fruit.

Place the jars on a stand in the preserving pan with a little water round. Cover and steam gently at 180°F for 10 minutes, and seal while hot. Care must be taken not to split the fruit. The fruit may be cooked in the vinegar before bottling, and the steaming process left out, if great care is taken not to split the skins.

Midnight feasts on one's own were dismal affairs, decided Hattie

AUNTIE'S NEENISH CAKES

1 lb ground almonds

¾ lb icing sugar

2 tablespoons flour

4 egg whites

Confectioner's custard (see below)

Soft icing (two colours)

Sift the almonds, sugar and flour together. Beat the whites until stiff. Add to the flour and mix to a very stiff paste. Line patty tins with the mixture and prick with a fork. Put on to a tray and bake in a moderate oven (Gas Mark 4, 350°F) until the pastry is just crisp. Make the confectioner's custard and fill the cases. Cover with two coloured icings, putting the first colour halfway across.

DAGO CAKES

½ lb flour

1 small teaspoon baking powder

A pinch of salt

¼ lb butter

¼ lb caster sugar

3 eggs

½ gill of milk and 1 tablespoon coffee essence

1 tablespoon cocoa

A few blanched almonds

Glacé cherries

Sift the flour, baking powder and salt. Cream the butter and sugar, add the well-beaten eggs, and lastly, the flour and most of the milk, alternately. Mix well. Take out one-third of the mixture and add the sifted cocoa to it, and an extra tablespoon of milk to the larger quantity. Quarter fill greased patty tins with the brown mixture. Put a small teaspoonful of the white mixture on top of each and pieces of almond and cherry on top. Bake for 10–15 minutes at Gas Mark 5 (375°F).

ROSE FAIRY CAKES

3 oz butter

3 oz sugar

2 eggs, separated

1 tablespoon milk

1 teaspoon rose water

5 oz flour

1 teaspoon baking powder

Salt

2 oz ground almonds

Carmine colouring

Cream the butter and sugar, add the beaten eggs, keeping one white for icing. Add the milk and rose water, and lastly, the sifted flour, baking powder, salt and almonds. Colour pale pink, and bake in a moderate oven (Gas Mark 5, 375°F) in deep patty tins, well greased, for 10–15 minutes.

The flavour of these cakes is better after a day. Cover with pale green icing and decorate with crystallized rose petals and cachous.

BLOATER BISCUITS

5 oz flour

½ teaspoon baking powder

¼ teaspoonful salt

Pinch of cayenne pepper

2½ oz butter

1½ oz bloater paste

1 egg yolk

Squeeze of lemon juice

Egg for glazing

Whipped cream

Sift the flour, baking powder, salt and cayenne. Rub in the butter and bloater paste well. Beat the yolk and lemon juice and add sufficient to make the mixture into a stiff paste. Roll out very thinly. Glaze with egg and bake in a moderate oven (Gas Mark 4–5, 350–375°F) for 10 minutes.

Mix together 1 teaspoon bloater paste and 1 teaspoon whipped cream. Spread a very little between 2 biscuits and serve as a savoury.

STEWED EELS

1 lb eels

½ teaspoon salt

1½ oz butter

1 oz flour

1 pint milk

1 dessertspoon chopped parsley

Pepper and salt

1 teaspoon anchovy essence

Wash eels in salt and water, put into a pan of cold water and bring to the boil. Drain and put into a basin of cold water. If the skin is not already removed, scrape off with the back of the knife.

Melt the butter in a thick pan, add the flour, and cook for a second or so; add the milk and stir until boiling. Cut the eel into neat pieces. Put into the sauce and cook very slowly for one hour. Add parsley, pepper and salt or anchovy essence. Serve on a hot dish. It is an improvement to add a tablespoonful of port wine.

O-LEVEL JAM TART

6 heaped tablespoons self-raising flour

2–2½ oz margarine

2 tablespoons water

Pinch of salt

About 4 oz jam

Make and roll the pastry as directed on p. 46. Cut off strips 1″ wide. Dampen the edge of a greased tart plate, and edge with the pastry strips. Roll the remaining pastry to fit the plate. Dampen the pastry edge and press on the circle. Cover with jam, leaving the outer rim of pastry clear. Decorate with curled strips of pastry, and bake on the second shelf of a fairly hot oven (Gas Mark 6, 400°F) for 30 minutes.

HORTENSIA'S SPECIAL BANNOCKS

½ lb medium oatmeal

½ lb flour

1 dessertspoon baking powder

1 teaspoon salt

1 oz margarine

1 oz sugar

1 egg

½ pint milk

Mix well together the oatmeal, flour, baking powder and salt. Rub in the margarine, distributing it evenly. Stir in the sugar. Beat the egg well. Make a well in the centre of the flour, pour in the beaten egg, then add the milk gradually to form a light dough. Form it quickly into 4 round cakes about ½″ thick and bake for 20 minutes on a greased tin in a very hot oven (Gas Mark 8, 450°F). Half these quantities will make 2 good-sized cakes.

MABEL'S EGGLESS NUTTIES

¾ cup flour

¼ teaspoon salt

2 cups rolled oats

½ cup sugar

½ cup chopped nuts and a handful of dried fruit

½ cup butter or clarified fat

1 teaspoon treacle

1 teaspoon bicarbonate of soda

Sift the flour and salt; add the oats, sugar, nuts and fruit. Melt the butter and treacle and stir into the dry ingredients. Add baking soda dissolved in 2 tablespoons boiling water. Drop in small pieces on a greased baking tray and bake at Gas Mark 3–4 (325–350°F) for 30 minutes.

Confectioner's Custard

½ pint milk

2 oz caster sugar

¾ oz flour

½ oz cornflour

1 egg plus 1 yolk

Vanilla flavouring

A knob of butter

Heat the milk in a saucepan. Whisk together the sugar, flour, cornflour and eggs until creamy. Beat in a little hot milk. Beat the mixture into the rest of the milk in the pan and cook gently, stirring, until thick and nearly boiling.

Stir in the vanilla flavouring and butter and cook, still stirring, for a moment longer.

Take off the heat and leave in a cold place to cool. Put a piece of greaseproof paper on the top to stop a skin forming.

Lettuce had occasion to wonder at Audrey's commitment to domestic science

BANANA FRITTERS

½ oz baking powder

3 oz flour

1 oz caster sugar

A little milk

3 bananas

Fat for frying

Mix the dry ingredients together, add sufficient milk to make into a very thin batter. Cut the bananas into small pieces, dip in the batter, fry in plenty of smoking hot fat, and drain on paper. Serve hot with sugar dredged over.

CHOCOLATE PUDDING

2 oz grated chocolate

2 oz butter or margarine

3 oz sugar

4 oz flour

½ oz baking powder

2 eggs, beaten

½ teaspoon vanilla essence

Melt the chocolate over boiling water. Butter a plain mould. Beat the butter and sugar to a cream. Stir in the flour and baking powder along with the eggs. Add the chocolate when cool. Lastly add the vanilla. Pour into the mould and steam for 2 hours.

EXAMINATION POTATO CAKES

½ lb cold cooked potatoes

¼ lb flour

1 oz lard or bacon fat

A little salt

½ teaspoon baking powder

Mash the potatoes and mix in the flour, fat, salt and baking powder. Work to a paste, roll out, cut into circles and cook either on a girdle or in a frying-pan; turn while cooking.

CHELSEA BUNS

1 lb self-raising flour

¼ teaspoonful salt

4 oz margarine or cooking fat

2 eggs, beaten

¼ pint milk or milk and water

6 tablespoons water

3 oz sultanas

3 oz sugar

Sieve together the flour and salt. Rub in the fat. Make a well in the centre of the flour and add the eggs. Mix to a smooth dough with milk and water. Turn out on to a floured board and knead a little. Shape into an oblong and roll out into a long strip about ¼″ thick. Sprinkle the fruit and sugar evenly over the surface, saving about a dessertspoonful of the sugar to sprinkle on the tops of the buns before baking.

Roll up firmly like a roly poly and cut into pieces about 1″ wide. Place on a greased baking sheet with the cut side up, and packed closely together to keep shape. Brush with a little milk and sprinkle with the remainder of the sugar. Bake for 15 minutes in a hot oven (Gas Mark 7, 425°F).

When cool, break the separate buns apart.

DOUGHNUTS 'MILLICENT'

6 oz flour

1 oz butter or margarine

2 oz caster sugar

¾ oz baking powder

1 egg

A little milk

Fat for deep frying

Put the flour into a basin, and rub the butter lightly into it. Add the sugar and baking powder and mix thoroughly. Beat up the egg and add it with sufficient milk to make a rather stiff dough. Roll out less than a ¼″ thick. Cut into rounds with a plain cutter (2½″ in diameter), then cut out the centre with a smaller cutter. Fry the circles in smoking hot fat till a light brown. Drain off the fat on paper, and dust over with caster sugar.

Makes 8–10 doughnuts.

RHODA'S RASPBERRY BUNS

3 oz butter or margarine

12 oz flour

1½ oz baking powder

3 oz caster sugar

1 egg

A little milk

Small quantity raspberry jam

Rub the butter lightly into the flour. Add the baking powder and the sugar. Beat the egg; stir it into the dry ingredients with sufficient milk to make a stiff paste. With floured hands form this mixture into balls. Make a hole in the centre of each with your finger, fill in with jam and cover over. Place on a greased baking sheet, flatten slightly, and bake in a hot oven (Gas Mark 6 or 7, 400–425°F) for about 12 minutes. Cool on a wire tray.
Makes 12 buns.

CSE SARDINE BALLS

12 tinned sardines

2 hardboiled eggs

1 dessertspoon butter

6 oysters

Salt and cayenne pepper

Lemon juice to taste

1 egg, beaten, plus extra for coating

2 tablespoons breadcrumbs, plus extra for coating

Flour for coating

Fat for deep-frying

Pound together the first 3 ingredients. Stir in the next 5. Form into small balls. Roll in flour, then in egg and breadcrumbs. Deep-fry in hot fat until golden brown.

Chapter 6

HOME FOR THE HOLS

Pig's Fry Bognor Regis
Gaylord's Fried Plaice
Boiled Sheep's Head
School Dinners' Special
  Lancashire Hotpot
Brian's Braised Beef
Rice Cutlets Frinton-on-Sea
Little Mo's Mixed Grills in the Oven
Lavinia's Liver Cakes
Southend Irish Stew
To Make Gravy
Brown Vegetable Sauce
Mrs Bignold's White Sauce
Sago Plum Pudding
Coconut Pudding Bellavista
Clacton Queen Pudding

Mrs Gledhill's Goosegog Crumble
Diplomatic Mould
Blackpool Brown Betty
Bananas as a Vegetable
Cabinet Pudding
Lords and Commons
Mrs Bignold's Daughter's Macaroni
  Pudding
Rokeby Pudding
Christmas Plum Pudding
Youth Hostel Apple Sponge Pudding
Maudie's Mince Pies
Whipped Cream Lowestoft
Nelson Pudding
Whipped Cream Kessingland

Home for the Hols

Did Mummie's cooking have that mouthwateringly Ah-Bisto aroma? Some mummies' did, others' didn't. Some mummies spent all day in the kitchen in flowery aprons with floury arms, mixing and rolling out. Their houses were full of singing – Mummie singing, the kettle singing on the hob, the canary singing in his cage – and the sweet warm smell of baking rising up the stairs and wafting under the children's bedroom doors and up their nostrils as they read their Enid Blyton books, golden hair shining under the anglepoise lamps. Then they would rush downstairs and scrape the mixture out of the bowl with a big wooden spoon (could something that tasted so nice really give you tapeworms?) and a bit later on there they were sitting round the fire with hot buttered scones and homemade strawberry jam from their own strawberry patch and steaming mugs of cocoa.

    Other households were not like that at all.

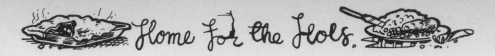

PIG'S FRY BOGNOR REGIS

About 1 lb pig's fry
Salt and pepper
A pinch of powdered sage
1 dessertspoon flour
1 Spanish onion
A little dripping
2 cooking apples
A little butter

Wash the fry well, put it in a stewpan with half a teaspoonful of salt, cover with water and simmer gently for 20 minutes. Drain, and when cold, dry with a clean cloth and cut in rather thin slices. Mix a seasoning of salt and pepper and the powdered sage with the flour. Dust the pieces of fry with this. Peel and slice the onion and fry it in a little dripping with the fry, until nicely browned. Place on a hot dish. Peel and slice the apples, and fry them in a little butter. Place them round the fry. Serve gravy separately.

GAYLORD'S FRIED PLAICE

Fillets of plaice
Seasoned flour
1 egg
Breadcrumbs (brown or white)
Fat for deep-frying

Wash the fish in cold water, dry well and dip into a little seasoned flour. Beat up the egg and brush the fish all over. Drain, and then place the fish in the breadcrumbs, pressing them on. Shake off any loose crumbs before placing the fish in the frying basket. Fry until golden, drain on soft paper, garnish with parsley and serve with pieces of lemon.

BOILED SHEEP'S HEAD

1 sheep's head
2 pints cold water
1 small bunch parsley
2 oz butter
2 oz flour
½ pint milk

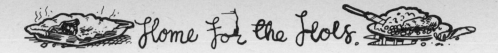

Salt and pepper

1 teaspoon powdered sage

Remove all the soft bones near the nostrils in the sheep's head, also take out the brain. Put the head and brain into a very large bowl of cold water with salt, and if possible, leave to stand overnight – if not, for at least 2 hours. Then wash the head thoroughly in cold water. Put into a large pan, cover with 2 pints cold water and allow to boil; simmer slowly for 2½–3 hours. The brain can be put in about 30 minutes before the head is cooked.

Take the head out, reserving the stock, and cut all the meat from the bones, skin the tongue and put all on a hot dish. Keep warm.

Chop the brain with the parsley; melt the butter, add the flour and cook for a minute, add the milk and reserved stock. Stir until boiling, then add pepper and salt, the brain and sage, and pour carefully over the meat.

If not wishing to serve hot, the meat may be chopped, and pepper, salt, sage and a little butter added, and the whole pressed into small buttered jars.

The kidney tartlets were not to everyone's taste

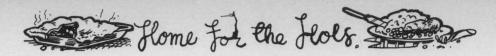
SCHOOL DINNERS' SPECIAL
LANCASHIRE HOTPOT

1 lb best end of neck of lamb or mutton

6 oysters (if liked)

1 small onion

1 lb potatoes, peeled and sliced

1 or 2 sheep's kidneys

Salt and pepper

½ oz dripping

Divide the meat into cutlets and put all the bones and lean trimmings, the beards of the oysters, and the onion, into a stew-pan; cover these with cold water, and boil them down into stock.

Grease a fireproof dish or casserole, line with a deep layer of the sliced potato, and on the top of that arrange the cutlets. On each cutlet place a slice of kidney and an oyster. Season well and cover with the rest of the potato. Pour down the side of the dish ½ pint of the hot stock, brush the upper layer of the potato with dripping, and bake for 2 hours in a moderate oven (Gas Mark 3, 325°F).

To make the top potatoes crisp and brown remove the lid 30 minutes before the dish is ready.

BRIAN'S BRAISED BEEF

2 rashers bacon

1 oz butter or margarine

2 lb top-side or silver-side of beef

Small head of celery

2 carrots

1 onion

1 turnip

¼ pint water or stock

Pepper and salt

1 bag herbs

Cut the bacon into squares and heat with the butter in a small pan. Brown the meat quickly on both sides. Remove the meat and fry the cut-up vegetables for a few minutes. Place the fried vegetables in a casserole with ¼ pint of water or stock, pepper, salt and the bag of herbs. Add the meat and cover with a closely fitting lid. Cook in the oven for 1½ hours at Gas Mark 2 (300°F).

Place the meat on a hot dish, strain the gravy round it and serve with vegetables cooked separately.

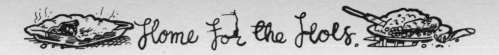

RICE CUTLETS FRINTON-ON-SEA

2 oz rice

¾ pint stock or water

1 small onion

¼ lb cooked meat, finely chopped

1 oz breadcrumbs

½ teaspoon chopped parsley

Salt and pepper

A little grated nutmeg if liked

Flour, egg and breadcrumbs for frying

Deep fat for frying

Fried parsley to garnish

Wash the rice and boil in the stock. Stir, and cook until the rice is soft and has absorbed all the liquid. Boil the onion separately and chop it very finely. Add the meat, breadcrumbs, onion, parsley and seasoning to the rice; mix thoroughly and cook for 2–3 minutes, then turn out on a plate to cool.

When cold, shape into small cutlets, flour, egg and breadcrumb each one, and fry in very hot deep fat until a light brown. Drain on paper. Serve on a paper doily and garnish with fried parsley.

Makes 10 cutlets.

— LITTLE MO'S MIXED GRILLS IN THE OVEN —

1 lb rump steak 1″ thick, or 2 small chops or cutlets

Sheep's kidneys

Liver, sliced

Sausages

Mushrooms and/or tomatoes

Seasoning

Caster sugar

Bacon

Butter, melted

Place the steak or cutlets and kidneys on a greased rack in a meat tin; the liver, sausages and mushrooms on a rack in another tin. Cut the tomatoes in halves with a sharp knife and sprinkle them with salt and pepper and a little sugar. Roll up the bacon and place in a tin with the tomatoes. Pour melted butter or margarine over the mushrooms. Bake in the oven for 15 minutes at Gas Mark 9 (475°F).

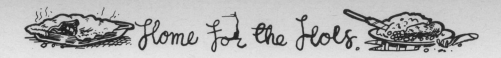

LAVINIA'S LIVER CAKES

4 rashers bacon

2½ cups minced liver

½ cup breadcrumbs

Salt and pepper

1 egg, lightly beaten

¼ cup stock or milk

fat for frying

Cut half the bacon into small pieces, add to the minced liver, breadcrumbs, salt and pepper, egg and stock or milk. Shape into flat, thin cakes and wrap in the remaining bacon cut into strips. Secure with cotton or wooden skewers. Put into a hot frying-pan with a little fat, cover and cook, turning frequently, for about 8–10 minutes. Serve hot with vegetables in season.

SOUTHEND IRISH STEW

2 lb neck or scraps of mutton

2 lb potatoes

2 onions

1 teaspoon salt

¼ teaspoon pepper

¾ pint water

Divide the meat into neat pieces, cut up the pieces, peel and cut up the potatoes roughly and slice the onions. Place in a casserole alternate layers of meat, potatoes and onions, with a good sprinkling of salt and pepper between the layers; pour in the water and cover tightly. Cook in the oven for 4 hours at Gas Mark ¼ (250°F).

TO MAKE GRAVY

1   After roasting a joint or bird, pour the fat out of the meat tin, leaving only the concentrated gravy.
2   Stir in 2 teaspoons flour and stir over heat until brown.
3   Add about ½ pint of stock gradually, boil, season, and strain if necessary.

Thick gravy can be made by leaving 2 tablespoons fat in the tin and adding 2 tablespoons flour and 1 pint stock.

'Gosh,' carolled Nesta, 'so that's what happened to my prune cake!'

BROWN VEGETABLE SAUCE

1 onion

A piece of turnip, carrot or swede

1 stick of celery or 1 small tomato

1½ oz dripping

A sprig of parsley

1 oz flour

½–1 pint of brown stock or water

Salt and pepper

Cut the vegetables into dice. Melt the dripping in a stout saucepan, add the vegetables and parsley. Cover with a lid and heat gently for 10 minutes. Remove the lid and stir occasionally for a further 10 minutes. Remove the vegetables with as little fat as possible. Add the flour, heat and stir until a good brown colour. Add ¼ to ½ pint of stock gradually, stir to a smooth sauce and boil, stirring all the time. Add the salt and pepper and cook for a few minutes.

Add the vegetables and more stock as required and leave to simmer gently for another 20 minutes. Strain and serve with mutton cutlets, fried steak or other meat dishes requiring a good brown sauce.

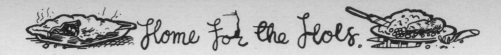

MRS BIGNOLD'S WHITE SAUCE

1 oz butter or margarine
1 oz flour
½–1 pint milk
Flavourings

Melt the butter in a saucepan, stir in the flour, add the milk, stir until smooth and boil for a few minutes, stirring the whole time. Add the flavouring desired.

This sauce is the foundation of White Vegetable Sauce, Parsley, Onion, Anchovy, Sweet Pudding and Egg Sauce, etc.

To ½ pint White Sauce add:
White Vegetable Sauce Salt and pepper to taste.
Parsley Sauce 2 teaspoons chopped parsley and salt and pepper to taste.
Onion Sauce 2 large onions chopped up and boiled until tender, with salt and pepper to taste.
Anchovy Sauce Salt, pepper and anchovy essence to taste.
Sweet Pudding Sauce 1 oz sugar and a few drops of flavouring essence.
Egg Sauce for Fish 1 hard-boiled egg, chopped, and salt and pepper.

SAGO PLUM PUDDING

4 tablespoons sago
2 small cups milk
1 teaspoon butter
½ cup sugar
1½ cups breadcrumbs
1 cup raisins, seeded
Essence of lemon
½ teaspoon baking soda
A pinch of salt

Soak the sago in the milk while preparing the other ingredients. Soften the butter in the sugar, and mix with the breadcrumbs, raisins, sago and milk. Add the lemon essence and baking soda, dissolved in 1 tablespoon boiling salted water. Mix well, put into a greased mould. Cover with greaseproof paper and steam for 2 hours.

Serve with sweet white sauce or custard.

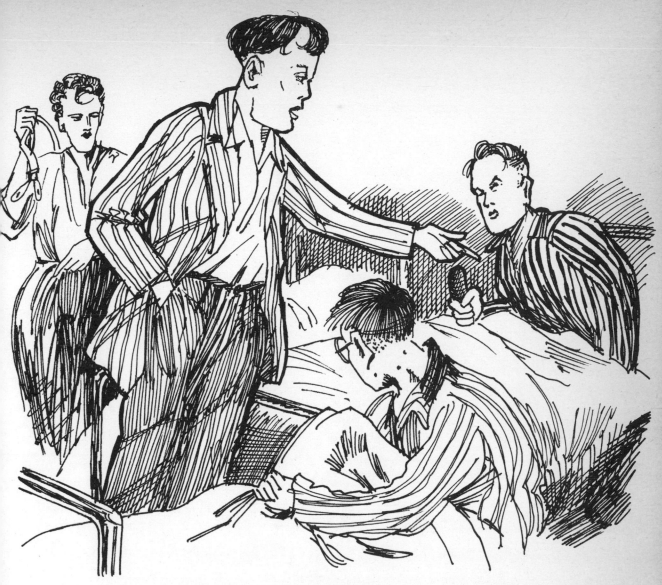

Hugo's knockwurst was the biggest in the dorm

— Coconut Pudding Bellavista —

1 pint milk
3 oz desiccated coconut
1 oz butter
3 oz breadcrumbs
1½ oz sugar
Grated rind of ½ lemon
1 egg, beaten

Boil the milk, pour it over the other ingredients mixed together in a bowl. Pour into a buttered pie dish. Bake in the oven at Gas Mark 6 (400°F) for 15 minutes.

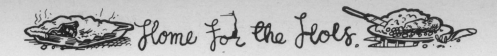

CLACTON QUEEN PUDDING

1 pint milk

Strip of lemon rind

4 oz white breadcrumbs

2 oz butter

1½ oz plus 2 oz sugar

2 tablespoons jam

2 egg whites

Put the milk and lemon rind in a pan and bring to the boil. Place the breadcrumbs, butter and 1½ oz sugar in a bowl, pour the boiling milk over, remove the lemon rind and allow to stand covered for 10 minutes.

When cooked, spread strawberry jam over the top. Whip the egg whites stiffly, fold in 2 oz sugar, and pile on top of the pudding. Brown lightly in the oven. This will take about 3–4 minutes at Gas Mark 6 (400°F).

MRS GLEDHILL'S GOOSEGOG CRUMBLE

1½ lb gooseberries

Sugar to sweeten

2 oz brown sugar

2 oz butter

4 oz plain flour

A pinch of cinnamon

Top and tail the gooseberries and put them in a pie dish with sugar to taste. Cover the dish and cook in the oven at Gas Mark 3 (325°F) for about half an hour until the juice starts to run out.

Rub the remaining ingredients together to look like breadcrumbs. Take the gooseberries out of the oven and turn it up to Mark 6 (400°F). Sprinkle the crumble mixture over the fruit. Put the dish in the oven for 20 minutes, when it should be crisp and golden on top.

Eat with cream or custard.

DIPLOMATIC MOULD

¾ oz gelatine

½ pint milk

1 oz sugar

Vanilla essence

2 oz glacé cherries, chopped

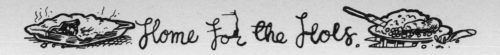

2 oz angelica

4 sponge cake fingers

1 tablespoon apricot jam

Small glass of sherry

1½ gills cream

1 stiffly whipped egg white

Dissolve the gelatine in the milk, add the sugar and vanilla, and allow to nearly set. Decorate a wetted mould with cherries and angelica. Spread the sponge cake with jam, and soak in sherry. Whip the cream and egg white. Fold together lightly and add to the milk.

Put a little mixture in the mould, then the sponge cake in the centre, followed by the rest of the mixture. Allow to set. Take care not to allow the sponge cake to show when the pudding is unmoulded.

BLACKPOOL BROWN BETTY

1 lb stale bread

1 lb cooking apples

A pinch each powdered cinnamon and ginger

2 oz demerara sugar

1 oz margarine

Stale bread is best for this. Grate it finely or rub through a sieve. Wash and core the apples, chop or grate them on a coarse grater. Mix the spices with the sugar. Put a layer of crumbs in a well greased pie dish, then a layer of apple, a sprinkling of sugar and spice. Repeat the layers, finishing with breadcrumbs. Put the margarine in flakes on the top and bake in a moderate oven (Gas Mark 6, 400°F) for 30 minutes.

BANANAS AS A VEGETABLE

2 bananas

Lemon juice

Brown sugar

1 tablespoon melted butter

1 tablespoon hot water

Salt

Peel the bananas and if they are thick cut in half lengthwise. Roll lightly in lemon juice and brown sugar and put in a buttered flat casserole. Pour over this the melted butter mixed with the water and a pinch of salt. Cook for 30 minutes at Gas Mark 5 (375°F).

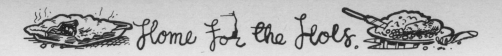

CABINET PUDDING

1 pint milk

½ gill sherry

4 egg yolks

2 egg whites

4 oz sponge cake

1½ oz caster sugar

A few ratafias

Cherries or angelica to decorate

Warm the milk and sherry, beat the yolks and whites together, stir in the milk quickly. Add the crumbled sponge cake, sugar and ratafias.

Grease a plain round cake tin and decorate it with cherries and angelica. Pour in the mixture and steam gently for an hour. Turn out on a hot dish and serve with wine or jam sauce.

LORDS AND COMMONS

A few stale sponge cakes

Two kinds of jam

Sherry

2 oz ratafia biscuits

1 pint milk

2 eggs, separated

1 oz cornflour

1 oz caster sugar

Flavouring of grated lemon rind

¼ pint whipped cream

Pink colouring

1 oz almonds

Cut up the cakes and make into sandwiches with the jam. Cut these into dice. Arrange them in a glass dish, and moisten with a little sherry, if desired. Distribute the ratafia biscuits amongst them. Make a custard with the milk, two egg yolks, the cornflour, sugar and flavouring (see p. 56). Pour this over the cake, level the surface and leave to cool. When cold, add the whipped cream to the beaten whites of eggs, and stir lightly together. Flavour and sweeten to taste. Colour half the cream mixture pink and ornament the top of the pudding with the pink and white creams. Decorate the edges with the blanched and shredded almonds.

'Nursie, Tittie's been acting awfully queer since she drank that tummy medicine . . .' mused Gertrude

Mrs Bignold's Daughter's Macaroni Pudding

2 oz macaroni

1 pint milk

1 oz sugar

A pinch of salt

1 egg

Break the macaroni into small pieces and soak for 1 hour or longer in the milk. Cook the macaroni and milk in a double saucepan until tender. Then add sugar and salt and turn into a greased pie dish. Add the well beaten egg and stir together. Bake for 40 minutes at Gas Mark 1 (275°F).

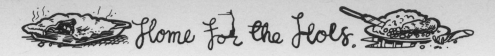

ROKEBY PUDDING

Jam Swiss roll (see p. 47)

2 oz ratafia biscuits

Stale bread

Stewed apricots or greengages

Creamy custard (see p. 56)

A few preserved cherries

The Swiss roll should be spread with apricot or plum jam before rolling. Cut the roll into thin slices. Line a plain mould with these, and fill in the spaces with the ratafia biscuits. Fill up the mould with alternate layers of sliced bread (crusts removed) and fruit. Cover the top with more slices of the roll, and if preferred the slices may be halved or quartered. Leave all night.

Turn out into a glass dish, and pour the custard (which should be flavoured with almond essence) over to coat it thoroughly, adding some mock cream if liked. Decorate with preserved cherries.

CHRISTMAS PLUM PUDDING

4 oz flour

1 oz baking powder

8 oz raisins

8 oz sultanas

1 oz mixed peel

8 oz suet

4 oz breadcrumbs

4 oz caster sugar

3 eggs

Milk to mix

1 lemon

1 glass brandy

Sift together the flour and baking powder and mix all the dry ingredients together. Beat the eggs well and stir in with sufficient milk to moisten. Add the grated rind and the juice of the lemon and the brandy. Make the mixture rather moist.

Steam in well greased pudding basin for 5 hours. Serve with a sauce.

White sauce Blend ½ oz cornflour with ½ pint milk, 1 oz butter and ½ oz caster sugar, and boil for 3 minutes, always stirring.

Clear wine or brandy sauce Blend ¼ oz cornflour with ½ pint water, and boil for 2 minutes, always stirring. Add ½ oz caster sugar and a glass of sherry or brandy.

The girls began to regret their curry powder prank at the staff luncheon

— YOUTH HOSTEL APPLE SPONGE PUDDING —

1 lb cooking apples

2 oz sugar

3½ oz butter or margarine

4 oz caster sugar

1 egg

6 oz flour

½ teaspoon baking powder

Peel and cut the apples, place in a pie dish, and add the sugar. Beat the butter and the caster sugar into a cream, add the egg, well beaten, a little at a time. Mix the flour and baking powder together and beat thoroughly with the butter mixture. Spread the mixture, which should be quite stiff, over the apples. Bake in the oven for 50 minutes at Gas Mark 4 (350°F).

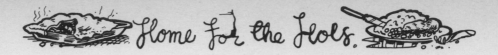

MAUDIE'S MINCE PIES

1 large apple, minced finely

2 tablespoons each sultanas, seedless raisins and currants

2 tablespoons sugar

Grated rind and juice of 1 lemon – more if liked

1 oz candied peel, finely chopped

½ teaspoon cinnamon

¼ teaspoon mixed spice

1 oz chopped nuts

1 teaspoon melted butter

1 tablespoon sherry or brandy

Shortcrust pastry (see p. 46)

Mix all the ingredients well together. Note: if brandy is used the mince will keep well.

Line greased patty tins with pastry; fill with mince; brush round the edges with water. Cover with pastry. Decorate the edges with a fork. Brush over with beaten egg. Bake at Gas Mark 6 (400°F) for about 15 minutes.

WHIPPED CREAM LOWESTOFT

(Using household milk powder)

(For trifles, flans, stewed fruit or sponge sandwiches)

¼ pint hot water

2–4 teaspoons sugar

1½ level teaspoons powdered gelatine

¼ teaspoon vanilla essence

3 heaped tablespoons household milk powder

2–4 oz margarine, melted

Put the hot water, sugar and gelatine into a large basin, and stir until the sugar and gelatine are dissolved. Add the vanilla and cool to blood heat. Sprinkle on top all the milk powder and whip briskly with a whisk or rotary type egg-beater for 10 minutes until the mixture becomes very stiff and increases in volume to 1–1¼ pints. Have ready the melted and cooled margarine, and add a tablespoonful at a time to the whipped mixture, beating each addition in thoroughly before adding the next.

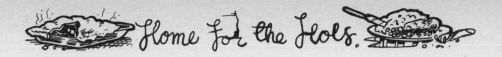

NELSON PUDDING

A few glacé cherries and a strip of candied peel

1 oz cornflour

½ pint milk

3 eggs, beaten

2 oz ratafia crumbs

2 oz breadcrumbs or cakecrumbs

½ oz baking powder

1 oz ground almonds

1 oz chopped suet

¼ oz chopped lemon rind

2 oz caster sugar

1 wineglass sherry

Butter a plain mould with clarified butter. Decorate with a few glacé cherries and strips of candied peel. Blend the cornflour with the milk, and boil for one minute. Take off the heat and let it cool for a few minutes. Stir in the beaten eggs, the crumbs (mixed well with the baking powder), ground almonds, suet, lemon rind, caster sugar and sherry. Place in the buttered mould and steam gently for 1 hour. Serve with apricot sauce poured round.

Apricot sauce Two tablespoons apricot jam, 1 dessertspoon caster sugar, ½ gill water, 1 glass sherry. Dissolve together, make hot, and strain round the dish.

WHIPPED CREAM KESSINGLAND
(Using evaporated milk)

1 level tablespoon gelatine

1 level tablespoon sugar

3 tablespoons hot water

1 tin evaporated milk

Dissolve gelatine and sugar in the hot water, stirring over a low heat until dissolved. (Do not allow to boil.) Pour the milk into a medium-sized bowl, add the cooled gelatine mixture, and whip with a rotary type egg-beater, whisk or fork until thick and fluffy (about 10 minutes).

'Well,' smiled Miss Fosdyke, 'we all know what happens when we don't eat our swede, don't we?'

Chapter 7

THE TUCK BOX

Gladys's Little Coffins
Ackroyd's Awful Athol Cakes
Spiffing Simnel Cake
Felixstowe Tart
Bath Buns 'Sixth Form Common Room'
Hot Cross Buns
Goosnargh Cakes
Doris's Derby Scones
Phyllida's Pumpkin Pie
Lemon Meringue Tart
Top-Hole Parkin
Lower Fourth Maids of Honour
Bakewell Tart
A Jolly Party Cake
Cheltenham Ladies' College Cherry Cake
Cousin Cuthbert's Madeira Cake
Après Lacrosse Sally Lunns
Justin's Jam Sandwich
Aunt Ada's Boiled Chocolate Fruit Cake
Hector's Eccles Cakes
Curry Sandwiches
Bloater Scones 'Deirdre'
Treacle Tart 'Head Girl'

The Tuck Box

The phrase 'Tuck in!', not much used today, is an invitation to gluttony. It brings to mind a Bunteresque figure, wider in the middle than elsewhere, with popping eyes starting through steamy round spectacles at a splendid array of cakes, jellies and trifles. A tuck box was a stout safe kept locked under the bed. Apart from confectionery bought at the tuck shop it was designed to hold larger items sent through the post by Mummie, fearful that her child was wasting away on a diet of three school meals a day. Things to send through the post, apart from delicacies from Harrods, would be large and solid like home-cured hams and sustaining fruit cakes. These were on no account meant to be shared with friends.

The latterday tuck box was the Tupperware lunch box. Tantalizingly see-through, it revealed the same combination of paste sandwiches and biscuits every day. Being suction-sealed in plastic gave the sandwiches a moist, easy-to-chew quality, and they were consumed with free milk, which children were forced to drink under threat of punishment.

GLADYS'S LITTLE COFFINS

3 egg yolks (large)

4 oz caster sugar

Beat the yolks and caster sugar together for 30 minutes or until very thick and stiff. Grease well small deep oblong patty tins (shaped like small coffins) and then dust lightly with flour. Half fill the tins with the mixture and bake very slowly for 30–40 minutes, starting at Gas Mark 3 (325°F) then turning the heat down to Gas Mark 2 (300°F). They should rise evenly, be hollow inside and a pale oak colour.

ACKROYD'S AWFUL ATHOL CAKES

5 oz flour

5 oz cornflour

1 teaspoon baking powder

6 oz butter

4 oz sugar

Grated rind of 1 lemon

3 eggs, beaten

2 oz chopped peel

A few chopped pistachio nuts

Sift the flours with the baking powder. Cream the butter and sugar with the grated lemon rind. Add the eggs and flour alternately, and mix well. Add the chopped candied peel, sprinkle with pistachio nuts, or coloured coconut. Bake in paper baking cups for 20 minutes at Gas Mark 5 (375°F).

It has to be said that these cakes are not at all awful, and it remains a mystery as to how they got their name.

SPIFFING SIMNEL CAKE

½ oz yeast

¼ pint of milk

½ lb warm flour

4 oz butter

3 egg yolks

1 teaspoon spice

4 oz sugar

4 oz candied peel

4 oz sultanas

4 oz currants

1 lb almond paste

Cream the yeast. Add the warmed milk. Pour into the flour, working in enough of the flour to form a sponge. Set to rise for 30 minutes. Mix in the rest of the flour, the creamed butter and the remaining ingredients, except the almond paste. Beat well, set to rise for 1–2 hours. Put half into a greased and floured tin. On this put one-third of the almond paste formed into a flat cake. Cover with the rest of the risen dough. Prove, then bake for 1–1½ hours at Gas Mark 5–6 (375–400°F).

When cold place a circle of the almond paste round the top. Mark this with a fork and place some small balls of almond paste round the top. Put into the oven at Gas Mark 2 (300°F) for 30 minutes to give it a light brown colour.

Decorate with crystallized fruits, Easter eggs, etc.

FELIXSTOWE TART

4 oz flour

4 oz cornflour

1 oz baking powder

4 oz butter or margarine

½ oz caster sugar

1 egg yolk

¼ pint milk or water

Filling

½ tin apricots or peaches, or jam

2½ oz sugar

2 egg whites

Angelica or preserved cherries

Mix together the flour, cornflour and baking powder. Rub in the butter lightly and add the ½ oz sugar. Beat the yolk of egg and milk together and stir into the dry ingredients. Make into a stiff paste and roll out. Butter the centre of a pie plate or side dish and wet the edges of it. Line the dish with the paste and crimp round the edge. Brush over with egg, mark with a fork and put into a hot oven (Gas Mark 4, 400°F) to bake for 30 minutes.

When baked, fill with the fruit or jam, and sprinkle 1 tablespoon of the sugar over. Beat up the egg whites to a stiff froth, stir in the remainder of the sugar and spread over the fruit. Decorate with strips of angelica or cherries or both. Place in the oven for about 5 minutes to brown lightly.

BATH BUNS
'SIXTH FORM COMMON ROOM'

½ oz yeast

2 oz sugar

½ gill milk or water

3 oz butter

½ lb flour

1 tablespoon sultanas or currants

½ oz chopped candied peel

1 large egg

A few comfits

Cream the yeast with 1 teaspoon of the sugar. Make the milk or water tepid, and add to the yeast. Rub the butter into the flour and add the fruits. Beat up the egg and add to the milk and yeast. Mix this into the flour, making a moderately firm dough. Divide into portions, shape into balls, and sprinkle with crushed lumps of sugar or comfits.

Place on a greased baking sheet. Bake for 15 minutes at Gas Mark 6 (400°F). Just before the cooking is completed, brush with beaten egg, and warm milk.

HOT CROSS BUNS

4 oz butter or margarine

1 lb flour

2 oz currants

4 oz caster sugar

¼ teaspoon salt

2 oz baking powder

1 level teaspoon ground cinnamon

1 level teaspoon ground mace

1 egg

½ pint milk

A small piece of pastry

Rub the butter into the flour. Add the currants, sugar, salt, baking powder and spices, and mix well. Beat the egg and add the milk to it. Mix this into the dry ingredients, making a moderately firm dough. Form into balls. Lay on a greased baking sheet. Roll out the pastry thinly, cut out crosses and put on top of the buns. Brush over with milk or egg and dust with sugar. Bake in a hot oven (Gas Mark 7, 425°F) for 15 minutes. Cool on a wire tray. Makes 12.

94

Nesbit noticed the pickle jar placed tantalizingly out of reach

GOOSNARGH CAKES

½ lb flour

2 oz sugar

A little salt

6 oz butter

1 egg yolk

1 teaspoon caraway seeds

Put all the ingredients into a bowl and work the mixture with the hand until all are mixed well together. Roll out on a floured board, knead slightly, cut into rounds with a cutter, and bake for 15 minutes at Gas Mark 5 (375°F). They should be a very pale brown; dredge with sugar when cooked.

'This is a citizen's arrest, Matilda,' cautioned Kimberley

DORIS'S DERBY SCONES

½ lb plain flour

½ lb wholemeal flour

2 oz sugar

½ teaspoon salt

1 teaspoon cinnamon

A little grated nutmeg

1 small teaspoon bicarbonate of soda

3 oz butter

1 egg

2 teaspoons cream of tartar

1 tablespoon golden syrup or treacle

1½ gills milk

Sift all the dry ingredients into a bowl, rub in the butter, add the egg, cream of tartar, syrup and milk to the flour, and make a soft dough. Knead slightly. Roll ½" thick, cut into rounds and bake on cold baking trays for 12 minutes at Gas Mark 7–8 (425–450°F).

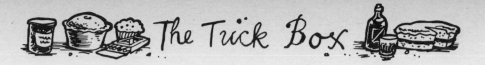

PHYLLIDA'S PUMPKIN PIE

½ lb shortcrust pastry (see p. 46)

Steam the pumpkin till tender. Rub through a sieve and to 1 pint of the pulp add:

2 eggs, well beaten

½ cup treacle or molasses

¼ lb brown sugar

2 tablespoons butter

½ cup milk

A pinch of salt

½ teaspoonful each of cinnamon and ginger

½ nutmeg grated

Mix well together. Line a pie plate with shortcrust. Pour in the mixture and bake for 30–40 minutes at Gas Mark 6 (400°F).

When cooked, spread a little whipped cream over the top or pipe it on just before serving.

LEMON MERINGUE TART

8 oz shortcrust pastry (see p. 46)

3 eggs

1 dessertspoon cornflour

½ pint milk

2 lemons

1½ tablespoons sugar

¼ teaspoon cinnamon

2 oz caster sugar

Line a greased sandwich tin with pastry. Separate the yolks from the whites. Blend the cornflour and some of the milk; bring the rest of the milk to the boil with the grated lemon rind. Stir in the cornflour. Boil, stirring well for 2 minutes. Add the 1½ tablespoons sugar, cinnamon, lemon juice and yolks. Pour into the sandwich tin and bake for 20 minutes at Gas Mark 6 (400°F).

Add the caster sugar to the stiffly beaten egg whites. Pile the meringue on top of the pudding and put back into the oven for about 3 minutes to brown and set the meringue.

It is probably asking for trouble to put this in a tuck box. But then, trouble is nice.

The Trick Box

TOP-HOLE PARKIN

½ teaspoon bicarbonate of soda

1 dessertspoon milk plus a little extra

½ lb oatmeal

¼ lb flour

A pinch of salt

1 teaspoon mixed spice

1 teaspoon ground ginger

6 oz brown sugar

¼ lb golden syrup or treacle

¼ lb butter or dripping

Split almonds

Dissolve the bicarbonate of soda in the dessertspoonful of milk. Mix together the oatmeal, flour, salt, spice, ginger and sugar. Heat the treacle and fat and mix with the oatmeal, adding the soda and milk, plus sufficient more milk to make a stiff mixture. Roll into balls, press on to a greased baking sheet, brush with milk and put split almonds on the top of each. Bake in the oven at Gas Mark 4 (350°F) for 15 minutes.

LOWER FOURTH MAIDS OF HONOUR

Pastry (see p. 46)

Filling

1 small floury baked potato

½ lb curd cheese

3 oz butter

2 egg yolks

3 oz caster sugar

Juice of ½ lemon

2 oz ground almonds

Grated lemon rind

½ glass brandy

A little grated nutmeg

Put the potato through a sieve and mix with the remaining ingredients for the filling. Line some patty pans with pastry, fill with the mixture and bake in a hot oven, Gas Mark 7 (425°F) for 10–15 minutes.

'Ah! Here's Bumstead with the main course,' enthused the Head

BAKEWELL TART

½ lb shortcrust pastry (see p. 46)

3 tablespoons jam

2 oz butter

2 oz caster sugar

1 egg

3 tablespoons breadcrumbs

2 oz ground almonds

Almond essence

Milk

Line a greased pie dish or sandwich tin with pastry and spread the bottom with jam. Beat the butter and sugar to a cream, add the egg and beat well. Then add the breadcrumbs and ground almonds together with the essence, and about 3 tablespoonfuls of milk. The mixture should not be too stiff. Pour over the jam and pastry. Bake at once for 40 minutes at Gas Mark 5 (375°F).

A JOLLY PARTY CAKE

8 oz margarine

8 oz sugar

5 eggs, beaten

10 oz self-raising flour

A pinch of salt

1 lb mixed currants and sultanas

½ lb raisins (or chopped prunes or dates)

½ teaspoonful almond essence, if desired

A pinch of bicarbonate of soda dissolved in 1 teaspoonful milk

Almond paste and royal icing (optional)

This recipe makes quite a large cake. Put the margarine into a mixing basin and beat it with a wooden spoon until soft, then add the sugar and beat until soft and creamy. Then add a little egg and a little flour (sieved with the salt) alternately, beating the mixture well. Continue adding egg and flour until all the egg and half the flour have been beaten into the mixture. Then gently stir in the remainder of the flour with all the fruit. Mix together, adding lastly the almond essence and the bicarbonate of soda dissolved in the milk.

Turn into an 8″ cake tin, lined with greaseproof paper brushed with melted margarine. Bake in the middle of a moderate oven (Gas Mark 4, 350°F) for 1 hour, then turn down to (Gas Mark 1, 275°F) and bake for a further 2¼ hours.

The next day, when cold, add almond paste and icing if required.

CHELTENHAM LADIES' COLLEGE
CHERRY CAKE

4 oz butter or margarine

4 oz caster sugar

4 eggs

4 oz flour

2 oz cornflour

4 oz glacé cherries

½ teaspoon grated lemon rind

½ oz baking powder

Butter and flour a 1 lb cake tin. Beat the butter and sugar to a cream. Add the eggs one by one, beating well. Mix the flour and the cornflour well together, and stir lightly into the batter. Cut the cherries in two, and add them. Last of all add the lemon rind and baking powder and mix lightly. Pour into the prepared tin, and bake in a moderately heated oven (Gas Mark 4, 350°F) for about 50 minutes. Turn out and cool on a wire tray.

—— COUSIN CUTHBERT'S MADEIRA CAKE ——

3 oz margarine

3 oz sugar

3 eggs, beaten

8 oz self-raising flour

A pinch of salt

Grated peel of 1 orange or ½ teaspoon vanilla essence

Put the margarine into a warmed basin, break it up with a wooden spoon and beat briskly until soft. Add the sugar and beat into the margarine, until the mixture is light and fluffy and looks like cream. Gradually beat in the eggs, one at a time, sprinkling in also a dessertspoonful of the sieved flour and salt. Beat each addition of egg thoroughly until all the egg is absorbed, and the mixture becomes thick and creamy.

Now gently fold in the rest of the sieved flour all at once with a metal spoon. Folding means lifting up the beaten mixture from the bottom of the basin and covering the flour with it. Then, with the edge of the spoon quickly cut through the mixture with several strokes and continue this lifting and cutting process until all the flour is folded in. Do not beat the mixture at this stage. Add the grated orange peel or vanilla essence towards the end of the folding process.

Line a cake tin with greaseproof paper. The paper for the side should stand up 1″ higher than the depth of the tin. Brush over with melted margarine. Pour in the mixture, levelling the top. Place on the middle shelf of a slow oven (Gas Mark 2, 300°F) and bake for 1¾ hours.

—— APRÈS LACROSSE SALLY LUNNS ——

1 lb flour

½ teaspoon salt

1 oz lard

1 oz butter

2 oz sugar

1 oz yeast

¼ pint warm milk

Put flour and salt into a bowl, rub in the lard and butter, add half the sugar. Cream the yeast with the rest of the sugar, add the warm milk, pour into the flour and knead well. Cover with a cloth and allow to rise for 1 hour.

Make into 2 round cakes, put on a greased baking sheet, prove 20 minutes, then bake for 20 minutes at Gas Mark 6 (400°F).

Brush over with a syrup made by boiling together 2 tablespoons sugar and 1 tablespoon cold water until it thickens.

JUSTIN'S JAM SANDWICH

6 oz flour

1 oz baking powder

A pinch of salt

4 oz sifted sugar

2 oz butter or margarine

1 egg

¼ pint milk

Essence of lemon, or other flavouring

Jam

Butter 2 round shallow baking tins. Mix the flour, baking powder and salt well together in a bowl. Beat the sugar and butter into a cream. Beat the egg separately, and add it to the sugar and butter. Work into this the mixture of flour, adding the milk and flavouring. Pour the mixture at once into the 2 tins and bake in a moderately hot oven (Gas Mark 5–6, 375–400°F) for 20–30 minutes.

When baked, turn out, cool on a wire tray, and sandwich together with jam.

AUNT ADA'S
BOILED CHOCOLATE FRUIT CAKE

(Melting method)

6 oz self-raising flour

½ teaspoon grated nutmeg

A pinch of salt

3 oz margarine

2 tablespoons sugar

1 tablespoon syrup

3 oz sultanas

2 heaped tablespoons cocoa

¼ pint hot water

½ teaspoon bicarbonate of soda

2 eggs, beaten

Sieve the flour, nutmeg and salt together. Put the margarine, sugar, syrup and sultanas in a saucepan. Blend the cocoa smoothly with the hot water, and add to the fruit mixture. Bring slowly to the boil and simmer for 3 minutes. Cool, and add the bicarbonate. Make a well in the centre of the flour. Pour in the mixture, add the beaten eggs, stir quickly, put into a greased, lined cake tin, and bake for 45 minutes in a moderate oven (Gas Mark 4, 350°F).

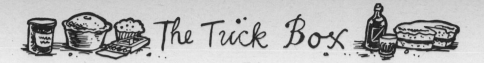
HECTOR'S ECCLES CAKES

4 oz shortcrust pastry (see p. 46)

6 oz currants

3 oz caster sugar

1½ oz finely chopped candied peel

½ teaspoon mixed spice

1 oz butter or margarine

A few drops of water

Divide the pastry into 8 pieces and roll out 4–5″ across. Mix the currants, sugar, peel and spices together. Put about a dessertspoonful of the mixture on to each round of pastry. Divide the butter into 8 pieces and put a piece on each round with a few drops of water. Moisten the edges of the pastry, draw them together over the top, flatten a little with the hand, turn over, and roll slightly. Make 3 or 4 cuts across the top. Bake for about 20 minutes in a hot oven (Gas Mark 6–7, 400–425°F).

Makes 8 cakes.

Rosina demonstrated a cunning way with used grapefruit halves

103

The Trick Box

CURRY SANDWICHES

Filling

Cold meat, finely minced

A little diced apple

1 teaspoon chutney

Squeeze of lemon juice

1 teaspoon curry paste or powder

Butter bread with chutney butter (butter creamed with salt, cayenne, lemon juice and a little chutney to taste).

Mix together all the filling ingredients, make the sandwich, and cut to shape.

BLOATER SCONES 'DEIRDRE'

½ lb self-raising flour

Salt, cayenne and lemon juice to taste

1–2 oz butter

2 oz bloater paste

1 egg, beaten

¾ gill milk

Sift together the flour, salt and cayenne. Rub in the butter and bloater paste. Add the egg, milk and lemon juice, and make into a soft dough. Knead slightly. Roll out ½″ thick. Cut into small rounds 1″ in diameter. Glaze with egg and bake at Gas Mark 7–8 (425–450°F) for 8–10 minutes.

TREACLE TART 'HEAD GIRL'

3 tablespoons syrup

1 tablespoon breadcrumbs

1 dessertspoon lemon squash (optional)

Pastry

6 heaped tablespoons self-raising flour

2–2½ oz margarine

2 tablespoons water

Pinch of salt

Make and roll the pastry. Mix together the ingredients for the filling, fill the tart and bake for 30–35 minutes at Gas Mark 4–5 (350–375°F).

104

Chapter 8

FIRESIDE TEA

Dunce's Brain and Bacon Soldiers
Scotch Collops
Pease Pudding
Après Hockey Fish Pudding
Pea Soup 'Ernestine'
Household Bread 80 Ivybridge Rd
Fish Paste 'Jim-Lad'
Baked Bean Toasts for the Boy Next Door
Pigtail's Potato Pie
Fruit Salad Brighton Pier
The Twins' Sweetbreads and White Sauce
Girl Friday's Fish Cakes
Hot Muffins
Mummie's Best Rissoles
Mersey Maisie's Sponge Cake
Toad-in-the-Hole
Trudy's Brains with Lemon Juice
Fireside Biscuits
Kirkcaldy Spatchcock
Eric's Own Tripe Casserole
Big Chief Bigfoot's Drop Scones
Dennis's Afternoon Tea Cakes

Fireside Tea

Eating tea on your lap in front of the fire with *Dr Who* on the television was a Saturday treat – other days tea was at the table with the television off. Or if it was on, the sound was turned down and you had to crick your neck to watch it.

Tea was a meal at which you might find almost anything from rissoles with gravy, fried onions and mashed potatoes, designed to fill the gap left by the uneaten school dinner, to boiled egg and soldiers. Sunday tea was the most predictable, with tinned salmon, a couple of lettuce leaves, half a tomato, a few spring onions and a blob of salad cream being followed by tinned peaches with evaporated milk and a jam and cream sponge cake.

Spam or corned beef were weekday alternatives to salmon, and in winter these could be served hot: the corned beef mixed with carrots in a shepherd's pie and the spam fried in egg-and-breadcrumbs to make the exotically named 'Vienna slice'.

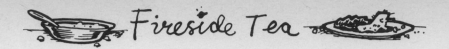

— DUNCE'S BRAIN AND BACON SOLDIERS —

Streaky bacon cut in thin strips to fit toast

1 set sheep's brains

1 egg, beaten

Salt, lemon juice, cayenne to taste

1 dessertspoon butter

Toast soldiers ½″ thick, 2″ long

Cook the bacon in the oven for a few moments, but do not shrink or curl it. Blanch the brains, skin and simmer for 10 minutes. Drain, add the beaten egg and seasonings. Melt the butter, add the mixture and cook gently till it thickens.

Put the bacon on the toast soldiers and pile the mixture on top.

—————— SCOTCH COLLOPS ——————

½ oz butter

1 teaspoon finely chopped onion

1 oz flour

½ pint stock or water

1 lb lean beef steak or 1 lb loin of mutton

Salt and pepper

1 slice toast

Parsley

Heat the butter in a pan and brown the onion. Next brown the flour and add the stock and the meat cut into small thin slices and without fat. Stir until boiling and then simmer gently for 45 minutes.

Season and serve in a hot dish with triangles of toast round. Garnish with parsley.

—————— PEASE PUDDING ——————

½ lb split peas

Salt and pepper

1 oz butter or margarine (optional)

1 egg (optional)

Wash the peas thoroughly and discard any black ones. Soak them in cold water overnight. Then put them in a cloth and tie rather loosely so that they have plenty of room to swell and plunge them into boiling water that has

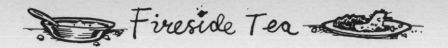

had ½ teaspoon salt added to it. Then boil until they are tender – about 2½ hours.

Take them out of the cloth and rub them through a coarse sieve. Season with salt and pepper, then tie tightly back in the cloth and boil for another 30 minutes.

If the pudding is to be served with pork or any boiled meat, it should be put in with the meat for the second boiling, as the broth will very much improve the flavour. If, however, the pudding is to be served alone, add the butter or margarine and a well-beaten egg after rubbing the peas through the sieve.

'It's just that some of us have contributed rather more than an oven cloth,' observed Chastity acidly

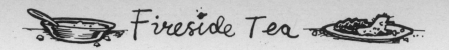

APRÈS HOCKEY FISH PUDDING

¼ lb salmon, or a small tin, or any white fish

½ pint unsweetened condensed milk

4 oz breadcrumbs, plus a little extra

4 oz butter

Salt and pepper

3 eggs, separated

Chopped gherkins, if desired

Flake and chop the salmon finely and stir in lightly the milk, breadcrumbs, melted butter, salt and pepper, and the beaten yolks of the eggs. Beat the mixture until creamy; stir in the stiffly beaten egg whites lightly. Grease a pudding mould and sprinkle it with fine breadcrumbs. Chopped gherkins added to the pudding add piquancy to the flavour.

Bake in the oven for 30 minutes at Gas Mark 5 or 6 (375–400°F). Alternatively, steam the pudding: cover it with greased paper and cook gently for 1 hour.

PEA SOUP 'ERNESTINE'

¼ lb split peas

1 oz bacon

2½ pints stock (water with bones added may be used)

½ carrot

½ turnip

1 onion

2 sticks celery

1 dessertspoon flour

Salt and pepper

1 dessertspoon dried mint

1 slice of toast

Soak the peas overnight, strain and add with the bacon to the stock. Bring to the boil and skim well. Wash and peel the vegetables. Cut up roughly. Add to the saucepan, and allow to simmer for 2–3 hours.

Pass the soup through a sieve. Add flour blended with water, salt and pepper and stir until boiling. Cook for 2 minutes. Rub the dried mint through a gravy strainer into the soup and serve with croûtons of fried bread or toast cut into small dice.

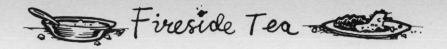

—— HOUSEHOLD BREAD 80 IVYBRIDGE RD ——

7 lb white flour

1¾ oz salt

2 oz yeast

1 teaspoon sugar

3½ pints warm water

Mix the flour and salt well together and warm in the oven. Cream the yeast and sugar until they become liquid, add the warm water, strain into the centre of the flour, mix and knead well. Put the dough into a clean, warm and floured basin and allow to rise for 1 hour in a warm place. Knead again.

Make into loaves and prove for 20 minutes or until risen. A 2 lb loaf should bake for 45–60 minutes at Gas Mark 5–6 (375–400°F).

—— FISH PASTE 'JIM-LAD' ——

3 red herrings

3 oz butter

1 egg

Pepper

Remove the skin and bone from the red herrings by pouring boiling water over them, and put them through a mincer. Melt the butter. Beat the egg well, and add to the melted butter. Add the herring. Stir well over a low heat till well mixed and hot, but do not boil. Season with pepper and put into pot while still hot.

—— BAKED BEAN TOASTS ——
—— FOR THE BOY NEXT DOOR ——

1 full-sized tin baked beans in tomato sauce

4 slices toast

2 oz cheese

1 teaspoon chopped parsley

A few grains of red pepper

Make the beans very hot and pile them on the toast. Sprinkle with the cheese finely grated, and brown lightly under the grill. Garnish with the parsley and red pepper.

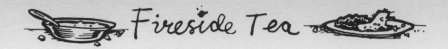

PIGTAIL'S POTATO PIE

¾ oz cornflour

1 pint milk

1 egg

Raw potatoes, thinly sliced

Grated cheese

Salt, pepper and made mustard

Mix the cornflour with a little of the milk to a smooth cream. Bring the rest of the milk to the boil and stir in the cornflour. Beat up the egg a little and stir in. Boil for 5 minutes, stirring all the time. Fill a well-buttered pie dish with alternate layers of thinly sliced potatoes and grated cheese, seasoning with made mustard, salt and pepper. Pour the above custard over it. Bake in a moderate oven (Gas Mark 4, 350°F) for 1 hour.

Serve accompanied with grated cheese on a separate dish.

FRUIT SALAD BRIGHTON PIER

1 lb mixed fresh fruit, such as cherries, strawberries, gooseberries, raspberries, currants, plums etc. according to the season

To which add any of the following:

4 oz prunes

1 oz almonds

A few pineapple chunks

1 tangerine orange

¼ tin apricots

2 bananas

Juice of 1 lemon

A few preserved fruits (if liked)

For the syrup

½ lb loaf sugar

½ pint water

Wine or liqueur flavouring (if desired)

Prepare all the fruits; stone the prunes, blanch the almonds, cut the apricots and pineapple into small pieces, divide the orange, slice the bananas. Put all together in a basin, and add the lemon juice.

Boil the sugar and water together for 15 minutes, cool and pour over the fruit. Add the apricot and pineapple syrup, and the wine or liqueur flavouring, if desired. Leave till cold. Serve in a salad bowl.

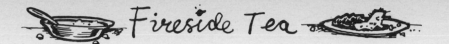

THE TWINS' SWEETBREADS
AND WHITE SAUCE

1 sweetbread

¾ pint stock or water

1 slice lean bacon

¼ pint white sauce (see p. 80)

Salt

A little lemon juice

Wash and soak the sweetbread for 30 minutes. Bring to the boil and drain. Put the stock, sweetbread and bacon into a saucepan. Simmer for 1 hour.

Heat the white sauce but do not boil. Season to taste with salt and lemon juice. Put the sweetbread into the sauce and re-heat.

Serve on a hot dish garnished with sippets of toast. For convalescents the sauce may be enriched by adding an egg yolk.

Nancy's tea parties owed little to tradition but were undeniably popular

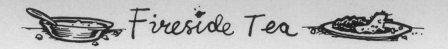

GIRL FRIDAY'S FISH CAKES

1 small tin salmon or 6 oz cold cooked fish

5 tablespoons liquid from the salmon, or water

1 heaped dessertspoon flour

1 heaped teaspoon chopped parsley

1 tablespoon tomato sauce

2 teaspoons vinegar

Pepper and salt

Milk

1 tablespoon dried breadcrumbs

Frying fat

Drain, bone and mash the fish, saving the liquid. Blend the flour smoothly with the liquid, and boil for 3 minutes, stirring continuously. Remove from the heat. Stir in the chopped parsley, tomato sauce, vinegar, fish and pepper and salt. Stir for a minute longer over the heat, then cool.

Form into 2 cakes on a floured board, brush with milk, coat with breadcrumbs and fry in hot fat until brown all over.

HOT MUFFINS

1 lb flour

2 oz baking powder

1 teaspoon salt

1 small teaspoon caster sugar

1 oz lard

½ pint milk

Mix the flour, baking powder, salt and sugar together well in a bowl. Rub in the lard. Make into a dough quickly with the milk, adding it a little at a time until you have a moderately soft dough. Do not knead more than is necessary.

Roll out flat on a floured board till about ½″ thick. With a circular cutter about 2–2½″ in diameter, cut into circles. Put these at once into a hot oven (Gas Mark 6–7, 400–425°F) or on to the griddle or hot plate, sprinkled with flour. They should be ready in 5–10 minutes.

Cut them open when hot, butter them and serve at once; or better, allow them to cool on a wire tray, cut them open, toast the insides, butter, and serve at once in a folded napkin, very hot.

Makes 12 muffins.

The girls disposed of Pauline's boiled cakes as soon as possible

MUMMIE'S BEST RISSOLES

4 oz cold cooked or tinned meat or sausage meat

1 medium-sized onion

½ oz cooking fat

1 heaped dessertspoon flour

5 tablespoons water

1 teaspoon meat extract

½ teaspoon Worcester sauce

Pepper and salt

1 tablespoon dried breadcrumbs

Mince or chop the meat. Fry the chopped onion in the cooking fat until soft. Stir in the flour, add the water and stir until the mixture thickens. Add the meat extract, Worcester sauce, pepper and salt and meat.

Leave to cool, and form into 2 rissoles on a lightly floured board. Brush with milk and coat with breadcrumbs and fry in hot fat on both sides. Serve with hot vegetables and gravy, or serve cold with salad.

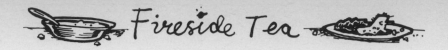

—— MERSEY MAISIE'S SPONGE CAKE ——

6 eggs

8 oz sifted caster sugar

Desiccated coconut or ground bitter almonds

8 oz cornflour

½ oz baking powder

Butter and flour a 2 lb cake tin. Beat the eggs, sugar and flavouring until thick and creamy. Mix the cornflour and baking powder well together. Sift it into the egg mixture very lightly and gradually, mixing with a fork or spoon. Pour at once into the prepared cake tin. which should be only half full, as this cake rises very high. Put at once into a hot oven (Gas Mark 7, 425°F) and bake for about 45 minutes.

Remove from the tin and cool on a wire tray.

—— TOAD-IN-THE-HOLE ——

¼ lb flour

2 eggs

½ pint milk

Salt

2 oz dripping

½–1 lb sausages

Make a batter of the flour, eggs, milk, and pinch of salt. Beat thoroughly, and, if possible, allow to stand for 2 hours before using. Make the dripping quite hot in a pie dish or baking tin, pour in the batter, drop the sausages in here and there, after removing the skins. Bake for 35 minutes in the oven at Gas Mark 7 (425°F).

N.B. Each sausage may be divided into 2 or 3 or left whole.

—— TRUDY'S BRAINS WITH LEMON JUICE ——

Calfs' brains

½ oz butter or margarine

½ oz cornflour

1 breakfast cup milk

¼ oz salt

2 small onions, grated

½ teaspoon chopped parsley

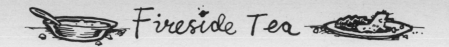

1 tablespoon lemon juice

Yolks of 2 eggs

The brains should be parboiled, and when cold veined and cut into small pieces. Melt the butter in a chafing dish, add the cornflour, and stir till smooth, gradually adding the milk. When smooth and boiling add the salt, onion, parsley, lemon juice and brains. Re-heat it, and when boiling, stir in the yolks of eggs and serve at once.

'Yow!' yelled Griffith, who wondered why he couldn't have a glass like everyone else

FIRESIDE BISCUITS

8 oz self-raising flour

A pinch of salt

3 oz margarine

2 tablespoons sugar

1 egg, beaten

4 tablespoons milk

Sift the flour and salt into a basin. Rub in the margarine. Add the sugar and mix with the egg and milk to a very stiff dough. Turn on to a floured board, and roll out very thinly. Prick all over with a fork, cut into rounds, and bake for 10–15 minutes on the second shelf of a moderately hot oven (Gas Mark 5, 375°F).

Makes 30–40 biscuits.

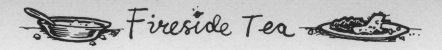

KIRKCALDY SPATCHCOCK

1 very young fresh chicken

Salt and pepper

1 tablespoon butter

1 teaspoon chopped parsley

½ teaspoonful finely minced onion

A few brown breadcrumbs

Cut the chicken in half down the backbone. Wipe and season inside and out with salt and pepper. Open out flat and keep in place with skewers. Brush over with melted butter and sprinkle with chopped parsley and onion.

Grill for about 20 minutes, turning frequently; just before it is done, sprinkle with the breadcrumbs and serve very hot with sauce (brown or tomato).

ERIC'S OWN TRIPE CASSEROLE

1 oz dripping

3 onions, sliced

1 oz flour

Pepper and salt

¾ pint water

1 lb tripe

½ teaspoon powdered sage

1 tablespoon Worcester sauce

Melt the dripping in a pan and brown the onions, add the flour, pepper and salt and brown these; add water and stir until boiling. Cut the tripe into 1″ squares, put into a casserole, pour the onion mixture over it, add the sage and Worcester sauce, put on the lid.

Cook at Gas Mark 1 (275°F) for 1–2 hours. When cooked, garnish with small triangles of thin toast.

BIG CHIEF BIGFOOT'S DROP SCONES

1 egg

1 gill sour milk

1 tablespoon sugar

6 oz flour

A pinch of salt

½ teaspoon cream of tartar

½ teaspoon bicarbonate of soda

Beat the egg and add the milk and sugar; sift the flour, salt, cream of tartar and soda together, then beat into the egg mixture to make a fairly stiff batter.

Drop in tablespoonfuls on a greased girdle or frying-pan, with the heat low. Cook till bubbles appear on the surface. Turn with a knife and brown the other side.

One dessertspoonful of syrup may be used instead of sugar; if no sour milk is available, use 1 teaspoonful of cream of tartar.

DENNIS'S AFTERNOON TEA CAKES

8 oz flour

¼ teaspoon salt

2 oz caster sugar

2 oz butter or margarine

2 oz currants

1 oz baking powder

2 eggs, beaten

A little milk

Mix together the flour, salt and sugar. Rub in the butter lightly. Mix in the currants and the baking powder. Stir in the beaten eggs with sufficient milk to make a smooth dough. Turn on to a floured board, and roll out ½″ thick. Cut into rounds, and bake in a hot oven (Gas Mark 6, 400°F) for about 15 minutes.

Cut the cakes open, butter, dust with sugar, and serve hot.

Makes 8–12 cakes.

'I know you're hiding the salami somewhere,' grated Miss Strangelove

Chapter 9

I DON'T FEEL VERY WELL

Invalid Mince
Gruel
Bread Trifle
Giblet Soup
Steamed Halibut or
 Whiting for Invalids
Barley Water
Egg Flip
Cup Arrowroot
Peptonized Milk
An Attractive and
 Body-Building Jelly
Junket
Tapioca Pudding
Sheep's Head Broth
Mutton Broth
Jellied Milk

Nourishing Lemonade
Plain Brown Soup
Albumen Water
Prune Jelly
Dr Arbuthnot's Salad
 for Convalescents
Toast Water
Steamed Eggs
Wayne's Wine Whey
Milk Soup
Prune Mould
Rusks
Coddled Apples
Nursery Pudding
Beef Tea
Meat Juice
Mutton and Veal Tea

I Don't Feel Very Well

The attractively named 'Sick Room' or 'Sick Bay' smelled of chloroform and was furnished with a hard camp bed with an enamel basin underneath it and rows of glass-fronted cupboards containing bottles of substances used in chemistry experiments. It was staffed by a lady in a white coat whose job it was to dispense the chemicals to the science mistress and to ply the sick with junior aspirins and bandages, according to whether the complaint was internal or external. Despite the lack of comfort, the Sick Room was a popular place. There was an aura of glamour about a girl who went regularly to the Sick Room – it was a declaration to those who understood, but only vaguely, that she had entered the mysterious realm of maturity. Another way of getting into the Sick Room was to stuff your fingers up your nose and hold your breath until you fainted and had to be carried there.

Sick children should be fed fortifying slops, bland food of neutral colouring that has been very thoroughly steamed or boiled. It should not require much effort in either mastication or digestion. Fresh orange juice should be placed near the bed of a sick child, gin and tonic for the older ones.

You can practise for the Sick Room at home by playing Doctor and Nurses.

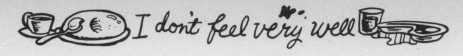

INVALID MINCE

¼ lb uncooked veal or chicken

1 slice onion

Water

¼ pint milk

½ oz butter

1 teaspoon flour or arrowroot

1 egg yolk (optional)

Salt and pepper

Mince for an invalid must be made with uncooked meat, as there is very little nourishment in meat that has been cooked twice. (Indeed nowadays it would be thought positively poisonous.) If you are using chicken, cut off one side of the breast of a fowl or chicken for the invalid before cooking the remainder for the family. For veal a piece of lean cutlet is best.

Cut the meat into very small pieces, removing all the skin. Shred the onion, put it in a saucepan with a tablespoonful of water, then add the milk and just simmer very gently for 5 minutes. Melt the butter in a saucepan, put in the meat and cook very gently for 3–4 minutes, but do not let it colour at all.

Strain the hot milk and pour it on to the meat. Mix the flour or arrowroot with a little cold milk until smooth, and stir it in. Cover closely and simmer very gently for 40 minutes, then stir in the well-whisked yolk of egg and a seasoning of salt and pepper. Stir for a few minutes, and then serve with sippets of toast. The success of this dish depends upon very slow cooking.

GRUEL

1 tablespoon oatmeal

1 pint milk

½ oz butter

1 teaspoon sugar

A little salt and nutmeg

Blend the oatmeal with a little milk, boil the remaining milk and pour it over the oatmeal, return to the pan, and stir until boiling. Allow to simmer for 20–30 minutes, then strain through a coarse strainer and add the butter, sugar, nutmeg and salt. Re-heat and serve.

'And we copied out the recipe too,' blushed Lesbia

Bread Trifle

2 large slices tin loaf

About 1 tablespoon strawberry jam

2 oranges

Water

½ pint custard

Use a sandwich or tin loaf and cut slices about ½″ thick. Remove the crusts and cut the bread in squares of four. Put half of them in a dish and spread with the jam, then put the remaining pieces on them.

Strain the juice from the oranges and add 2 tablespoons hot water. Make it hot without boiling and pour it over the bread, cover and leave to soak. The custard can be made with powder or egg (see p. 56) – but whichever is used, flavour it by infusing the yellow part of the orange peel in the milk. Put it in a saucepan with the orange peel and leave over very low heat until it is nicely flavoured, then pour it over the trifle.

This is a very useful recipe for using up stale bread. It is a very wholesome dish, too, and most children love the combined orange and strawberry flavour. Tangerines with marmalade are also good.

GIBLET SOUP

2 sets giblets

1 onion

1 carrot

¼ head of celery

1 turnip

Bunch of herbs

2 cloves

1 blade of mace

6 peppercorns

2 quarts stock

1½ oz butter

1½ oz flour

Caramel, if needed

1 gill wine or sherry, if liked

Lemon juice, if liked

Salt and pepper

Clean and scald the giblets, then drain. Prepare the vegetables, put in a saucepan with the giblets, herbs and spices and stock. Simmer for 2 hours, then strain and remove the fat.

Brown the butter slightly in a saucepan, add the flour, stir until smooth and golden; add the strained soup, and stir till boiling. Cut the best pieces of the giblets and add to the soup. Simmer for 20 minutes. Skim from time to time.

Add some caramel if not brown enough, the wine or sherry or a squeeze of lemon juice. Salt and pepper to taste.

STEAMED HALIBUT OR WHITING
FOR INVALIDS

1 halibut

Salt and pepper

Lemon juice

Butter

White sauce (see p. 80)

Wash the halibut and dry it. Place in a buttered pie dish to which have been added 3 tablespoons water. Sprinkle with salt, pepper and lemon juice. Dot the top with small pieces of butter and cover with greased paper. Cook on the middle shelf of a moderate oven (Gas Mark 4, 350°F) for about 20 minutes. Mask with white sauce.

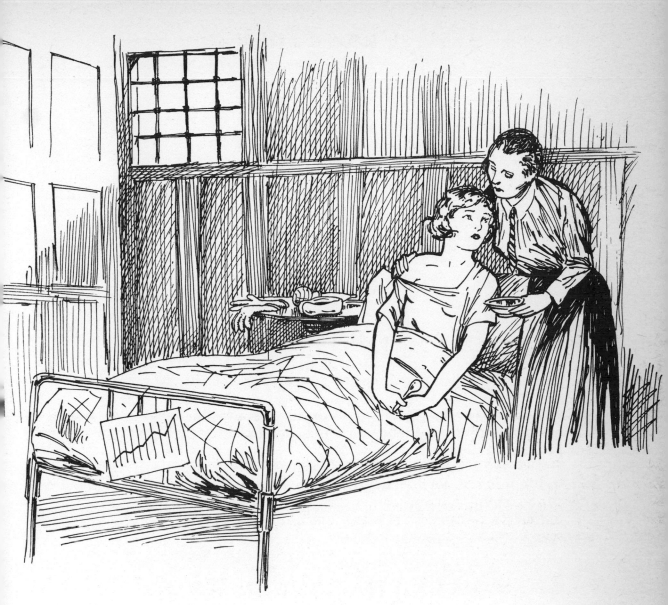

Oriel found matron's bedside manner comfortingly attentive

BARLEY WATER

2 oz pearl barley
A little salt
1 quart water
Strip of lemon rind

Wash the barley and put into a pan with the salt, water and lemon rind. Allow to boil, then simmer slowly for 2 hours. Strain and use as required.

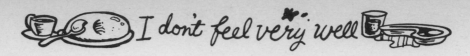

EGG FLIP

½ pint warm milk
1 egg
1 teaspoon sugar
1 tablespoon sherry or brandy

Heat the milk, separate the yolk from the white of the egg, mix the yolk and sugar well together; pour the warm milk over this, then allow to cool. Whip the white of the egg stiffly, add to the other ingredients with the brandy, and serve in a tumbler.

CUP ARROWROOT

1 teaspoon arrowroot
½ pint milk
1 egg, beaten
1 teaspoon sugar

Blend the arrowroot with a little of the milk and put the remainder on to heat. Add the arrowroot to the milk, and stir till boiling. Cook for 2 minutes. Allow to cool slightly. Add the beaten egg and sugar and cook without boiling. Serve in a dainty bowl.

PEPTONIZED MILK

1 pint milk
1½ gills cold water
2 teaspoons Benger's liquid pancreaticus
¼ teaspoon bicarbonate of soda
A little salt

Heat the milk and water gently, add the pancreaticus, soda and salt, and stand in a warm place for 15–20 minutes, or until the milk tastes nutty. Boil up or place on ice to arrest the peptonizing process.

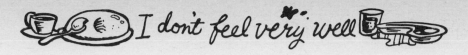

AN ATTRACTIVE AND
BODY-BUILDING JELLY

Fruit jelly (see p. 23)

Ovaltine rusks

Jam or lemon cheese

1 gill whipped cream

Angelica and cherry to decorate

Make the jelly, sandwich the rusks with jam or lemon cheese between. Place neatly in a glass dish. Pour the warm jelly over to just cover them. Let it set. Decorate with cream piped through a rose pipe, and candied fruit. Fresh fruit may also be set in the jelly.

'Now *will you try an hors d'oeuvre?' Venetia nervously implored*

JUNKET

1 pint milk

1 dessertspoon sugar

A little flavouring

1 teaspoon essence of rennet or ½ rennet tablet

Heat the milk to blood heat (98°F). Dissolve the sugar in it and add the flavouring. Add the rennet, stir in well, and put into a dish or custard glasses to set. Do not disturb while setting. Any flavourings may be used.

If a rennet tablet is used, crush and dissolve it in 1 teaspoonful of cold water. Junket sets quicker in a warm place.

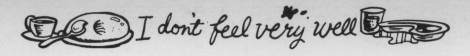

TAPIOCA PUDDING

2 oz tapioca

1 oz sugar

1 pint milk

A little grated nutmeg

¼ oz butter or shredded suet

Wash the tapioca and put into a pie dish with the sugar, milk and nutmeg, stir well, then add the butter or shredded suet. Bake slowly at Gas Mark ½–1 (250–275°F) for 2½–3 hours.

Note: After 1 hour, add extra milk if necessary. The tapioca may be boiled till soft before baking.

SHEEP'S HEAD BROTH

1 sheep's head

2 oz pearl barley

2 quarts cold water

1 each: carrot, turnip, onion, leek

8 peppercorns

1 teaspoon salt

1 dessertspoon chopped parsley

Wash the head well, and remove all the slimy parts, also the inside of the nostrils. Soak well in salt water for 2 hours, wash again. Cook with barley and water for 1½ hours.

Cut all the vegetables into dice and add to the head, with the peppercorns and salt. Simmer for 30 minutes longer. Then remove the head and serve the broth, garnished with parsley, and the tongue, skinned and cut into small pieces.

MUTTON BROTH

2 lb scrag end of neck of mutton

1 carrot

1 turnip

1 large onion

Small bunch of herbs

6 peppercorns

Salt and pepper

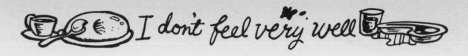

1 tablespoon pearl barley

3 pints cold water

Wash the meat, cut in small pieces, and put it in a stew-pan. Prepare the vegetables and slice them, tie the herbs and peppercorns in a piece of muslin. Add these to the meat, also a teaspoonful of salt, a sprinkling of pepper, the barley and the water.

Bring to the boil, skim, then simmer gently for 1½ hours. Skim well.

To serve as a meal, the meat may be left in and, if liked, potatoes can be added 20–30 minutes before the meat is done, according to size.

To serve as a first course, strain the soup, skim well, and if liked, add some of the vegetables and barley, or sprinkle on a little finely chopped parsley.

JELLIED MILK

½ oz powdered gelatine

3 tablespoons water

2 tablespoons cream

½ pint milk

6 lumps of sugar

Vanilla essence to taste

Soak the gelatine in the water. Beat the cream, add the milk to it. Add the sugar to the water and gelatine and dissolve over heat. Cool, but before it sets add it gradually to the cream and milk. Add the vanilla essence. Pour the mixture into a basin, stirring well now and then until it is just beginning to set, then leave until cold. Stirring prevents the cream from rising to the top. If a doctor orders it, a little brandy or rum may be substituted for the vanilla essence and will improve the flavour.

NOURISHING LEMONADE

Rind of 3 lemons

6 oz lump sugar

Juice of 4 lemons

1½ pints boiling water

4 eggs

½ pint sherry

Wash and peel the lemons very thinly; put the peel into a bowl, add the sugar and strained lemon juice and pour the boiling water over. Whip the eggs, and when the mixture is quite cold add these and the sherry. Strain and use.

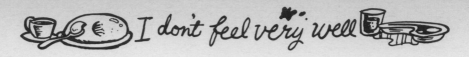

I don't feel very well

PLAIN BROWN SOUP

1 carrot

1 onion

1 turnip

1 quart stock

Jelly from under the dripping, or if not, Bovril

1 oz oatmeal

Small bunch of mixed herbs tied up in muslin

About 1 teaspoon gravy browning

Salt

Cut the vegetables into dice. Bring the stock to the boil, put in the jelly, oatmeal and herbs. Boil gently until the vegetables are tender.

Skim the stock, add the colouring. Season to taste. Remove the herbs before serving.

ALBUMEN WATER

White of 1 fresh egg (not more than 12 hours old)

1½ gills (¾ of a breakfast cupful) of filtered water, or water which has been boiled and allowed to get cold, with a pinch of salt

Whip the white very slightly – just enough to break it up; put in a screw-topped jar with the water and shake it thoroughly to blend. If ordered by the doctor, a small quantity of brandy may be added. A large tumbler, covered with thick paper or cardboard, will do instead of a jar. In cases of vomiting, albumen water will often remain on a very irritable stomach.

PRUNE JELLY

1 lb prunes

2 pints water

2½ oz cornflour

2 oz caster sugar if prunes are not very sweet

Stew the prunes in a little of the water from the 2 pints until soft, which will take about 15 minutes. Remove the stones and pound up the rest of the fruit in a mortar. Mix the cornflour to a smooth cream with a little of the water. Bring the rest of the water to the boil and stir the cornflour and the sugar into it. Add the pounded prunes and boil for 8 minutes. Allow to cool.

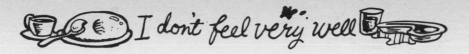

DR ARBUTHNOT'S SALAD
FOR CONVALESCENTS

Crisp heart of lettuce
Slices of pineapple
1 lb tomatoes or pimentos
Small tin of asparagus tips
¼ lb cream cheese
9 walnuts, broken into pieces
Salt, cayenne, lemon juice
Mayonnaise

Place a border of small crisp lettuce leaves round a plate and a round of pineapple with the centre removed in the middle. Cut long narrow spears of half the tomatoes or pimentos and place between the lettuce leaves, radiating from the edge of the pineapple to the outside of the plate. Place the asparagus tips on the pineapple, radiating from the centre. Chop the remaining tomatoes or pimentos roughly. Mix with the cream cheese and walnuts. Flavour with salt, cayenne and lemon juice. The mixture should be a delicate pink. Neatly pile the mixture in the centre of the pineapple and in little mounds round the edge. Serve the mayonnaise separately.

'Ah good, the junket poultice,'
muttered sinister Doctor Arbuthnot

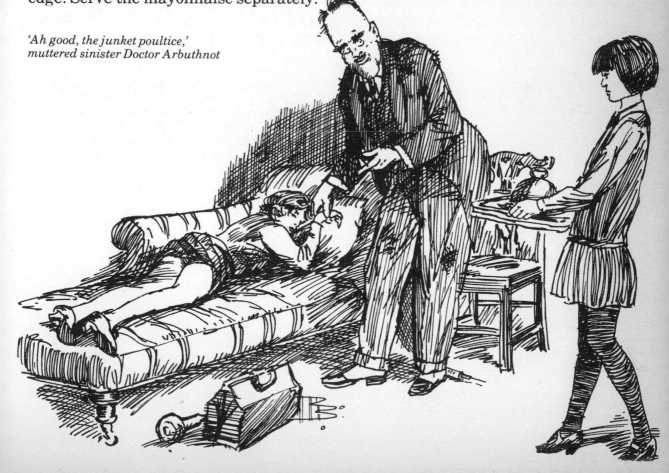

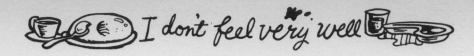

TOAST WATER

(To quench the thirst and clean the tongue in cases of fever)

1 crust of bread weighing 2 oz

1 pint filtered water

Toast the crust slowly until very brown. Soak in the water until it turns bright amber. Strain through muslin.

STEAMED EGGS

Eggs

Pepper and salt

Butter a saucer or scallop shell. Break a fresh egg into the centre and put pepper and salt on. Cook over boiling water for 11–15 minutes. If allowed, very tiny strips of streaky bacon may be placed in the white before steaming.

WAYNE'S WINE WHEY

½ pint milk

2 tablespoons sherry

A little sugar

Heat the milk to almost boiling point; add the sherry, and allow to stand to curdle. Boil again, strain, sweeten, and serve.

MILK SOUP

½ oz cornflour

1 pint best milk

A pinch of salt

½–¾ oz caster sugar

Blend the cornflour to a smooth cream with a little of the milk. Put the rest of the milk into an enamelled saucepan with the salt and sugar, and bring to the boil. Remove from the fire and add the cornflour, stirring until quite smooth. Boil for 10 minutes, stirring all the time, and serve.

For flavouring, add a stick of cinnamon or a bay leaf to the milk, removing it after boiling the cornflour. To make the consistency of a gruel, use ¾–1 oz cornflour.

'I'm most awfully sorry,' blurted Mibsy, 'I've burnt the semolina again!'

PRUNE MOULD

4 oz prunes

½ pint boiling water

1 pint of liquid made up of juice from prunes and water

4 level tablespoons cornflour or arrowroot

3 tablespoons syrup or sugar

½ teaspoon lemon essence

Soak the prunes overnight in ½ pint boiling water. Transfer prunes and water to a saucepan and simmer gently until soft. Drain, save the liquid and make it up to 1 pint with water.

Stone and chop the prunes. Blend the cornflour with a little of the liquid; boil the rest of the pint and stir into the blended cornflour. Return to the saucepan, add the syrup, cook for 3 minutes, then add the prunes and lemon essence, stirring continuously. Pour into a wetted mould and leave to set.

RUSKS

1 lb self-raising flour

½ teaspoon salt

6 oz butter, or ½ butter and ½ lard

2 eggs

½ cup milk

1 dessertspoon sugar

Sift the flour and salt. Rub the butter in. Add the beaten eggs and milk gradually. Roll out ½″ thick. Cut into rounds, and bake in a fairly hot oven (Gas Mark 6, 400°F) until pale brown (10–15 minutes).

Split in halves, return to the oven at Gas Mark 3 (325°F) and brown very slowly for 20 minutes.

Made with any recommended diabetic flour and without the sugar, these rusks would be suitable for diabetic patients.

CODDLED APPLES

1–2 cups white or brown sugar

2 cups boiling water

8 apples

Lemon juice

Make a syrup by boiling the sugar and water for 5 minutes. Core and pare the apples; cook slowly in the syrup; cover closely and watch carefully.

When tender, lift out the apples, add a little lemon juice to the syrup and pour it over the apples. The cavities may be filled up with jelly or raisins.

NURSERY PUDDING

1 lb apples

2 oz demerara sugar

Thin slices bread

Grated lemon rind

1 pint packet lemon blancmange powder

Stew the peeled and cored apples (windfalls will do quite well) with sugar to taste. Cut the bread in fingers, put a layer in a buttered pie dish, then a layer of stewed apples and a little grated lemon rind. Three parts fill the dish with these layers and pour in the syrup from the fruit. Make the blancmange according to directions and spread it on the top.

This may be served cold or made hot in the oven.

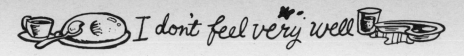

BEEF TEA

1 lb buttock or rump steak

1 pint cold water

A pinch of salt

Scrape the steak across the grain, put into a jar with the water and salt and allow to stand, covered, for 30 minutes, stirring frequently. Then cover with a greased paper, tie down, and steam in the oven at Gas Mark 1 (275°F) for 3–4 hours.

Strain through a coarse strainer and serve with fingers of toast, if the patient is permitted these. Pepper should be used only with the permission of the doctor.

BEEF TEA

(Quick method)

Ingredients

As above

Scrape the meat across the grain and put into a basin with the cold water and salt. Allow to stand, covered, for 30 minutes, stirring frequently. Stand in a saucepan containing 2″ water, stir, and allow to simmer gently for 30 minutes.

Strain, remove the fat, and serve.

MEAT JUICE

Make a small quantity of beef tea as above. Allow to stand for 45 minutes, but do not cook. Serve in a ruby glass.

MUTTON AND VEAL TEA

½ lb fillet veal

½ lb fillet mutton

1 pint cold water

A little salt

Prepare and cook as Beef Tea.

'I'm not sure I want to see your speciality, actually,' mumbled Reginald

METRICATION

WEIGHT

1 oz	28.35 g
2 oz	56.7 g
4 oz	113.4 g
8 oz	226.8 g
12 oz	340.2 g
16 oz	435.6 g

Note: For convenience round off metric measures to the nearest 25 g.

LIQUIDS

¼ pint (1 gill)	142 ml
½ pint	284 ml
1 pint	586 ml

TEMPERATURES

	Gas Mark	Fahrenheit	Centigrade
Cool	¼–½	250	121
Very slow	1	275	135
Slow	2	300	149
Very moderate	3	325	163
Moderate	4	350	177
Moderately hot	5	375	191
	6	400	205
Hot	7	425	218
Very hot	8	450	232
	9	475	246

ACKNOWLEDGEMENTS

I would like to thank Sarah Rennie
for her immaculate typing.
L.S.

I would like to thank the artists –
mostly anonymous – whose work I
have cannibalized, cut up, and
otherwise corrupted.
T.E.